colorSTYLE

Innovative to traditional,
17 inspired designs to knit

PAM ALLEN & ANN BUDD

INTERWEAVE
INTERWEAVEBOOKS.COM

colorSTYLE

Innovative to traditional,
17 inspired designs to knit

PAM ALLEN & ANN BUDD

INTERWEAVE
INTERWEAVEBOOKS.COM

PHOTOGRAPHY: **Carol Kaplan**
COVER AND INTERIOR DESIGN: **Jillfrances Gray**
TECHNICAL EDITING: **Karen Frisa**
ILLUSTRATION: **Gayle Ford**

Interweave Press LLC
201 East Fourth Street
Loveland, CO 80537-5655 USA
interweavebooks.com

Printed in China by Asia Pacific Offset.

Library of Congress Cataloging-in-Publication Data

Allen, Pam, 1949-
Color Style : Innovative to traditional, 17 inspired designs
to knit / Pam Allen and Ann Budd, authors.
p. cm.
Includes bibliographical references and index.
ISBN 978-1-59668-062-3 (pbk.)
1. Knitted. 2. Knitting–Patterns. 3. Color in art. I. Budd,
Ann, 1956- II. Title.
TT825.A453 2008
746.43'20–dc22

2008008686

10 9 8 7 6 5 4 3 2 1

ACKNOWLEDGMENTS

Color Style is the sixth book in the Style series, and once again, we count ourselves fortunate indeed to work with so many talented people. Their creativity, enthusiasm, and hard work contribute beyond measure to the quality of each book.

For their colorful projects, we thank designers: Véronik Avery, Chrissy Gardiner, Cecily Glowik, Mags Kandis, Marta McCall, Robin Melanson, Mary Jane Mucklestone, Deborah Newton, Kristin Nicholas, Shirley Paden, Mari Lynn Patrick, and Jaya Srikrishnan. Without these dedicated knitwear designers, there would be no book.

Thanks to photographer Carol Kaplan for taking pictures that enhance the beauty of these knitted projects and to her assistants, Denise LeBreux and Jefferson White.

We're grateful to Carrie Hoge for her invaluable help with styling; to make-up artist Leslie Tracy for her skillful work; to Susanna Crampton at Historic New England for letting us shoot at Gropius House in Lincoln, Massachusetts; to David Moore for his gracious welcome; and to models Caitlin FitzGerald, Lealyn MacAlister, and Lauren FitzGerald.

Thanks to Karen Frisa, our tech editor, for her meticulous pattern instructions; to Veronica Patterson, copy editor, for smoothing out our words; to Gayle Ford for her beautiful illustrations; and to Jillfrances Gray, whose design for the series looks fresh with each new book.

CONTENTS

The patterns will give you new ways to think about knitting with two or more colors.

COLOR YOUR WORLD

Color. It's everywhere—from the subtle grays and browns of a winter landscape to the bold primaries of modern art. Fortunately for knitters, yarns come in almost any color imaginable, and there's no end to the ways they can be combined in colorwork stitches. From simple projects in variegated or handpainted yarns to intricate intarsia designs that use dozens of colors, you can find as many ways to add color to your knitting as you can find colors to choose from. But many knitters hesitate when it comes to working with two or more colors because they lack a solid foundation in colorwork techniques or because they don't trust their ability to combine colors.

Following the format of the other books in the popular Style series (*Scarf Style, Wrap Style, Lace Style, Bag Style,* and *Folk Style*), *Color Style* is a book about knitting with color as well as a book of colorful projects to knit. It's a collection of patterns from fourteen talented and inventive knitwear designers, each of whom has incorporated two or more colors into knitted fabric in a fresh, innovative way. Every design offers an individual lesson in inspiration, application, technique, and, of course, style. As a collection, the patterns will give you new ways to think about knitting with two or more colors and provide you with endless creative possibilities for creating your own colorful masterpieces.

Whether you're new to knitting with multiple colors or are already comfortable knitting stripes, mosaics, Fair Isle, and intarsia—as well as adding embellishments—be sure to take in the Design Notebook that begins on page 116. You'll find clear explanations and helpful tips for the most-frequently used color-work techniques, and you'll see how the contributing designers used them to their best advantage.

If you're a beginning knitter, don't worry. The Glossary of Terms and Techniques at the end of the book includes illustrated instructions for all the specific techniques mentioned in the projects. Along with the easy-to-follow directions and clear illustrations in the project and design chapters, the glossary will provide all the help you need to successfully complete any project in this book.

colorPATTERNS

For this mismatched-stripes pullover, **Mary Jane Mucklestone** took inspiration from the quilts of Gee's Bend, particularly the strip quilts worked in the Lazy Gal pattern. She based the muted color palette on a narrow range of corduroy colors used in women's work from the 1970s. Both back and front are constructed from three panels of mismatched stripes; different stripe sequences are used for the narrow set-in sleeves. After the strips are sewn together, stitches are picked up from the provisional cast-on, and the lower body edging is worked downward in garter stitch with an opening left at the side seams for a loose fit. The garter-stitch neckline is shaped with strategically positioned decreases.

STITCH GUIDE

Color Sequence for Right Front and Left Back Panels

4 rows rust, 4 rows brown, 4 rows dark brown, 4 rows green, 4 rows rust, 4 rows brown, 4 rows green, 4 rows dark brown, 4 rows green, 4 rows brown, 2 rows green, 2 rows brown, 2 rows green, 2 rows dark brown, 2 rows green, 2 rows brown, 4 rows green, 2 rows brown, 2 rows dark brown, [16 rows brown, 2 rows dark brown, 2 rows rust, 2 rows dark brown, 10 rows rust] 1 (2, 2, 2) time(s), 16 rows brown, 2 rows green, 6 rows brown, 2 rows dark brown, work to end in brown.

Color Sequence for Left Front and Right Back Panels

4 rows rust, 2 rows dark brown, 4 rows rust, 6 rows dark brown, 2 rows green, 6 rows dark brown, 2 rows brown, 2 rows dark brown, 4 rows brown, 2 rows dark brown, 4 rows brown, 4 rows green, 4 rows brown, 2 rows green, [4 rows brown, 4 rows dark brown, 2 rows brown, 4 rows dark brown, 2 rows rust, 8 rows brown, 2 rows rust] 1 (2, 2, 2) time(s), 6 rows brown, 2 rows rust, 4 rows brown, 6 rows rust, 2 rows green, 8 rows rust, 2 rows brown, 2 rows rust, work to end in brown.

FINISHED SIZE
About 36 (39½, 44, 48)" (91.5 [100.5, 112, 122] cm) bust circumference. Pullover shown measures 36" (91.5 cm).

YARN
Worsted weight (#4 Medium).
Shown here: Classic Elite Princess (40% merino, 28% viscose, 10% cashmere, 7% angora, 15% nylon; 150 yd [137 m]/50 g): #3438 noble nutmeg (brown; MC), 4 (5, 6, 7) skeins; #3476 baronet's brown (dark brown) and #3425 tawny chestnut (rust), 2 skeins each; #3460 greatest green, 1 (1, 2, 2) skein(s).

NEEDLES
Body and sleeves—size U.S. 7 (4.5 mm). Edging—size U.S. 6 (4 mm): 24" (60 cm) circular (cir). Adjust needle size if necessary to obtain the correct gauge.

NOTIONS
Small amount of waste yarn for provisional cast-on; markers (m); stitch holder; tapestry needle.

GAUGE
17 stitches and 28 rows = 4" (10 cm) in stockinette stitch on larger needles.

Sew together panels of
mis-matched stripes.

Color Sequence for Right Sleeve

8 rows rust, 6 rows brown, 4 rows green, 2 rows dark brown, 6 rows rust, 2 rows dark brown, 6 rows brown, 4 rows green, 4 rows dark brown, 14 rows brown, 2 rows dark brown, 2 rows rust, 6 rows brown, 2 rows green, 14 rows brown, 4 rows dark brown, 2 rows brown, 2 rows dark brown, 4 rows brown, 2 rows dark brown, 20 rows brown, 2 rows green, work to end in brown.

Color Sequence for Left Sleeve

Work as for right sleeve, but switch rust and green stripes throughout.

> **NOTE**
> ❖ The front and back are each made in three separate panels that are sewn together.

BACK CENTER PANEL

With rust, larger needles, and using the provisional method (see Glossary, page 133), CO 36 sts. Beg with a RS row, work in St st stripes as foll: 4 rows rust, 2 rows green, 2 rows rust, 10 rows green, 2 rows dark brown, 10 rows brown, [6 rows green, 2 rows dark brown, 8 rows brown, 4 rows rust, 2 rows dark brown, 4 rows brown, 4 rows rust] 1 (1, 2, 2) time(s), 2 rows green, 12 rows rust, 2 rows dark brown, 10 rows brown, 2 rows rust, 4 rows brown, 2 rows dark brown, 2 rows brown, 2 rows dark brown—piece measures 14 (14, 18¼, 18¼)" (35.5 [35.5, 46.5, 46.5] cm) from CO. Cont in brown until piece measures 20¼ (22¼, 24¼, 25¼)" (51.5 [56.5, 61.5, 64] cm) from CO, ending with a WS row. BO all sts.

FRONT CENTER PANEL

CO and work as for back center panel through end of stripe sequence (2 rows dark brown), then cont in brown until piece measures about 15¾ (17¾, 19¾, 20¾)" (40 [45, 50, 52.5] cm) from CO, ending with a WS row.

Shape Neck

(RS) Cont with brown, k10, join new ball of yarn and BO center 16 sts, knit to end—10 sts rem each side. Working each side separately, BO 2 sts at each neck edge 4 times—2 sts rem each side. BO all sts.

RIGHT FRONT AND LEFT BACK PANEL (MAKE 2)

With rust, larger needles, and using the provisional method, CO 23 (27, 32, 36) sts. Work in St st foll the color sequence for right front and left back panels (see Stitch Guide) and *at the same time*, when piece measures 13 (13½, 15, 15½)" (33 [34.5, 38, 39.5] cm) from CO, shape armhole.

Shape Armhole

Cont in stripe sequence, BO 4 (4, 6, 6) sts at beg of next WS row, then BO 2 (3, 3, 5) sts at beg of foll 2 WS rows—15 (17, 20, 20) sts rem. Cont even until armhole measures 8 (9½, 10, 10½)" (20.5 [24, 25.5, 26.5] cm), ending with a RS row.

Shape Shoulder

BO 5 (6, 7, 7) sts at beg of next 3 (2, 2, 2) WS rows, then BO 0 (5, 6, 6) sts at beg of foll WS row—no sts rem.

LEFT FRONT AND RIGHT BACK PANEL (MAKE 2)

With rust, larger needles, and using the provisional method, CO 23 (27, 32, 36) sts. Work in St st foll the color sequence for left front and right back panel (see Stitch Guide) and *at the same time*, when piece measures 13 (13½, 15, 15½)" (33 [34.5, 38, 39.5] cm) from CO, shape armhole.

Shape Armhole

Cont in stripe sequence, BO 4 (4, 6, 6) sts at beg of next RS row, then BO 2 (3, 3, 5) sts at beg of foll 2 RS rows—15 (17, 20, 20) sts rem. Cont even in stripe patt until armhole measures 8 (9½, 10, 10½)" (20.5 [24, 25.5, 26.5] cm), ending with a WS row.

Shape Shoulder

BO 5 (6, 7, 7) sts at beg of next 3 (2, 2, 2) RS rows, then BO 0 (5, 6, 6) sts at beg of foll RS row—no sts rem.

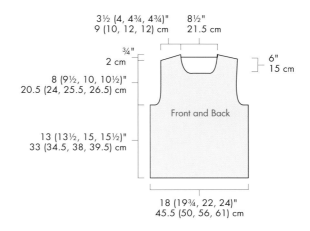

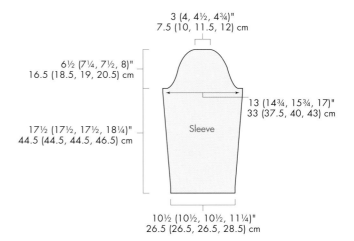

SLEEVES

With dark brown and smaller cir needle, CO 45 (45, 45, 48) sts. Do not join. Work in garter st until piece measures 2" (5 cm) from CO, ending with a WS row. Change to larger needles. Work in St st foll the color sequence for sleeves (see Stitch Guide) and *at the same time* inc 1 st each end of needle every 8th row 5 (9, 11, 12) times—55 (63, 67, 72) sts. Cont even until piece measures 17½ (17½, 17½, 18¼)" (44.5 [44.5, 44.5, 46.5] cm) from CO, ending with a WS row.

Shape Cap

BO 3 (3, 5, 5) sts at beg of next 2 rows, then BO 2 (3, 3, 5) sts at beg of foll 2 rows—45 (51, 51, 52) sts rem. Dec 1 st each end of needle every other row 7 (7, 4, 2) times—31 (37, 43, 48) sts rem. Dec 1 st each end of needle every 4th row 5 (6, 8, 10) times—21 (25, 27, 28) sts rem. Dec 1 st each end of needle every other row 4 times—13 (17, 19, 20) sts rem. BO all sts.

FINISHING

Weave in loose ends. With brown threaded on a tapestry needle, sew the right front and left front panels to the center front panel, being careful to follow a column of sts on each piece. Sew the right back and left back panels to the center back panel in the same manner. Sew sleeve caps into armholes. Sew sleeve and side seams.

Neckband

With dark brown, smaller cir needle, and beg at left shoulder, pick up and knit 91 sts around front neck and 36 sts across back neck—127 sts total. Place marker (pm) and join for working in rnds. Purl 1 rnd, knit 1 rnd, purl 1 rnd. *Dec Rnd 1:* K20, pm, k2tog, k8, pm, k2tog, k27, ssk, pm, k8, ssk, pm, k20 (you'll be at the left front shoulder), k10, pm, k2tog, k12, ssk, pm, k10—121 sts rem. Purl 1 rnd, knit 1 rnd, purl 1 rnd. *Dec Rnd 2:* [Knit to m, k2tog] 2 times, [knit to 2 sts before m, ssk] 2 times, knit to m, k2tog, knit to 2 sts before m, ssk, knit to end of rnd—115 sts rem. Purl 1 rnd. BO all sts kwise.

Waistband

Beg at right front side seam, remove waste yarn from provisional CO around entire lower edge and carefully place live sts on smaller cir needle—158 (174, 194, 210) sts total. With dark brown, sl 1, pm for beg of rnd, *knit to last st of panel, k2tog (last st of panel and first st of next panel); rep from * 5 more times—152 (168, 188, 204) sts rem. Purl 1 rnd, then knit 1 rnd, then purl 1 rnd. Work front and back separately as foll: K76 (84, 94, 102) front sts, place rem 76 (84, 94, 102) sts on holder to work later for back. Working back and forth in rows, work in garter st (knit every row) for 20 rows. BO all sts. Return 76 (84, 94, 102) back sts to needle and work in garter st for 20 rows to match. BO all sts.

Weave in rem loose ends. Steam-block thoroughly.

Stripes do not have to be symmetrical— let serendipity be your guide!

Jaya Srikrishnan took inspiration from India's annual springtime Holi Festival (Festival of Colors) for these riotously colorful mitts. A highlight of the Holi festival is the moment when participants toss dyes and water at each other, resulting in brightly tinted clothing and skin. Jaya chose three colorways of handpainted yarn—one that changed from bright to muted, one that changed from light to dark, and one that had a few complementary colors—to mix with a coordinating solid color. Worked in a simple slip-stitch pattern, the colors appear as specks, bands, and blotches in interesting ways. Jaya used variegated shades of warm reds and yellows in these mitts, but the concept would work just as well with disparate colors.

NOTES

✦ To avoid a ladder of loose stitches at the boundaries between double-pointed needles, be sure to tension the last stitch of each needle tightly. Check frequently that the transition between rounds is smooth and has the same elasticity and appearance as the rest of the fabric.

✦ Do not cut the yarns at the end of rounds when working the charted patterns; simply drop them, then pick them up again when needed. The next yarn to be used is always the one that has not been used for the longest time. Pick up the yarn farthest away from the needles.

✦ If the thumb gusset needs to be lengthened after working the Gusset chart (because the end of the gusset does not reach the crook of your thumb), work as many rounds of Additional Gusset chart as desired (continue to work Hand chart on other stitches).

✦ Use the tail of yarn from the beginning of the thumb to close up any holes that might occur at the join between the gusset and the thumb.

✦ To help prevent possible holes from forming at the base of the thumb, pick up an extra stitch (or two or three) when beginning the thumb. Decrease the extra stitches on the following round.

FINISHED SIZE
About 7¼ (7½, 8½)" (18.5 [19, 21.5] cm) hand circumference and 7 (7½, 8)" (18 [19, 20.5] cm) total length. Mitts shown measure 7½" (19 cm).

YARN
Fingering weight (#1 Super Fine).

Shown here: Lorna's Laces Shepherd Sock (80% superwash wool, 20% nylon; 215 yd [197 m]/2 oz): #37ns violet (A), #107 red rover (B), #401 neon (C), and #38 mixed berries (D), 1 skein each.

NEEDLES
Size U.S. 1 (2.25 mm): set of 4 or 5 double-pointed (dpn). Adjust needle size if necessary to obtain the correct gauge.

NOTIONS
Markers (m); small amount of waste yarn for holding gusset sts; tapestry needle.

GAUGE
38 stitches and 74 rows = 4" (10 cm) in slip-stitch pattern, worked in rounds.

Use variegated
yarn to add color
complexity to a simple
slip-stitch pattern.

MITT

With A, CO 68 (72, 80) sts. Place marker (pm) and join for working in rnds, being careful not to twist sts.

Cuff

Work in k2, p2 rib for 30 rnds—piece measures about 2¾" (7 cm) from CO. Join other colors as needed and work Rnds 1–10 of Hand chart.

Thumb Gusset

M1 (see Glossary, page 137), pm, work to end of rnd in patt as established—1 gusset st between 2 markers. Working the gusset st (inc as indicated) according to Gusset chart, cont working rem 68 (72, 80) sts according to Hand chart until there are 23 (27, 31) gusset sts bet markers. If a longer gusset is desired, work the gusset sts according to Additional Gusset chart (see Notes). Place 23 (27, 31) gusset sts on waste yarn to be worked later for thumb.

Hand

Pm and rejoin for working in rnds—68 (72, 80) sts. *Note:* Pull the working yarn tight to ensure that the join on the inside of the thumb stays firm. Keep firm tension on the yarn in this area for the next few rounds. Cont in patt as established until piece measures about 6¼ (6¾, 7¼)" (16 [17, 18.5] cm) from CO, or about ¾" (2 cm) less than desired total length, ending with Rnd 2, 12, 22, or 32 of chart. Cut off all colors except A.

Top Edge

With A only, knit 1 rnd. Work in k2, p2 rib for 5 rnds. Knit 10 rnds. Loosely BO all sts.

Thumb

Arrange 23 (27, 31) held gusset sts on dpn. Join A and knit these sts, then pick up and knit 1 st at the base of the hand sts—24 (28, 32) sts. (Pick up extra sts if necessary to prevent holes from forming in this area—see Notes.) Work in k2, p2 rib for 5 rnds. Knit 10 rnds. Loosely BO all sts.

FINISHING

Weave in loose ends, using nearby tails to close any holes at base of thumb (see Notes). Block lightly if desired.

Gusset

(chart rows) 33, 31, 30 ← end size 7½", 29, 27, 26 ← end size 7¼", 25, 23, 21, 19, 17, 15, 13, 11, 9, 7, 5, 3, 1

Slip-stitch patterns obscure the straight boundaries between knitted stripes.

Hand

(chart rows) 39, 37, 35, 33, 31, 29, 27, 25, 23, 21, 19, 17, 15, 13, 11, 9, 7, 5, 3, 1

Additional Gusset

 1

	with A, knit
	with A, purl
=	with B, knit
·	with B, purl
+	with C, knit
·	with C, purl
□	with D, knit
·	with D, purl
×	with color used in rest of rnd, knit
V	sl 1 wyb
M	M1
□	pattern repeat

MOHAIR FAIR ISLE

MARI LYNN PATRICK

Mari Lynn Patrick borrowed motifs from the Middle East—one from Turkey and one from Egypt—and combined them with traditional Fair Isle patterns in this comfy casual sweater. The Turkish *kilit* (lock) pattern, which represents the lock to a lover's heart, is commonly used on socks. Here it trims the bell cuffs of the sleeves. The large motif in the center of the yoke appears on many acient Egyptian artifacts. In an unusual twist on yoke construction, the front half of each upper sleeve is worked along with the front yoke and the back half of each sleeve is worked along with the back yoke. Mari Lynn worked different color patterns on the front and back yoke. The shoulders are shaped in the center of each sleeve.

NOTES

✤ Different colors are used for the Fair Isle pattern on the yoke back and front.

✤ The yoke is worked in two sections—the back plus half of each sleeve and the front plus half of each sleeve. The tops of the sleeves are seamed at the end.

FINISHED SIZE
33 (37, 41, 45)" (84 [94, 104, 114.5] cm) bust circumference. Sweater shown measures 37" (94 cm).

YARN
Worsted weight (#4 Medium).

Shown here: Classic Elite La Gran Mohair (76.5% mohair, 17.5% wool, 6% nylon; 90 yd [82 m]/42 g): #63588 peach blossom (MC), 7 (7, 8, 9) balls; #61555 tangerine, #6516 natural, #6562 blue spruce (dark teal), #6525 sunflower (bright yellow), #6552 eggplant, #61530 periwinkle, and #6572 underappreciated green (chartreuse), 1 ball each.

NEEDLES
Body and sleeves—size U.S. 9 (5.5 mm): straight and 24" (60 cm) circular (cir). Edging—size U.S. 8 (5 mm): straight. Adjust needle size if necessary to obtain the correct gauge.

NOTIONS
Markers (m); smooth waste yarn or stitch holders; tapestry needle.

GAUGE
16 stitches and 21 rows = 4" (10 cm) in stockinette stitch on larger needles; 17 stitches and 20 rows = 4" (10 cm) in charted pattern on larger needles.

Let the halo on mohair yarn soften color boundaries.

BACK

With MC and smaller needles, CO 66 (74, 82, 90) sts. *Next row:* K2, *p2, k2; rep from *. Cont in k2, p2 rib as established for 5 more rows—piece measures about 1" (2.5 cm) from CO. Change to larger straight needles and cont in St st for 10 rows, ending with a WS row.

Shape Waist

Dec row 1: (RS) K11 (12, 13, 14), place marker (pm), sl 1, k1, psso, k10 (11, 12, 13), pm, sl 1, k1 psso, k16 (20, 24, 28), k2tog, pm, k10 (11, 12, 13), k2tog, pm, k11 (12, 13, 14)—62 (70, 78, 86) sts rem. Work even in St st for 5 rows. *Dec row 2:* (RS) Knit to first m, sl 1, k1, psso, knit to next m, sl 1, k1, psso, knit to 2 sts before next m, k2tog, knit to 2 sts before last m, k2tog, knit to end—4 sts dec'd. Rep the last 6 rows 3 more times—46 (54, 62, 70) sts rem. Work even for 11 rows, ending with a WS row. *Inc row:* (RS) Knit and *at the same time* inc 1 st after the first 2 markers and inc 1 st before the last 2 markers—4 sts inc'd. Work 5 rows even. Rep the last 6 rows 3 more times, then rep inc row once more—66 (74, 82, 90) sts. Work even until piece measures 14½ (15, 15½, 16)" (37 [38, 39.5, 40.5] cm) from CO, ending with a WS row.

Shape Armhole

BO 4 sts at beg of next 2 rows, then BO 1 st at beg of next 4 (6, 8, 8) rows—54 (60, 66, 74) sts rem. Slip sts onto larger cir needle and set aside.

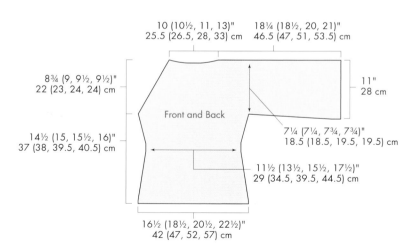

10 (10½, 11, 13)"
25.5 (26.5, 28, 33) cm

18¼ (18½, 20, 21)"
46.5 (47, 51, 53.5) cm

8¾ (9, 9½, 9½)"
22 (23, 24, 24) cm

11"
28 cm

Front and Back

14½ (15, 15½, 16)"
37 (38, 39.5, 40.5) cm

7¼ (7¼, 7¾, 7¾)"
18.5 (18.5, 19.5, 19.5) cm

11½ (13½, 15½, 17½)"
29 (34.5, 39.5, 44.5) cm

16½ (18½, 20½, 22½)"
42 (47, 52, 57) cm

FRONT

CO and work as for back. Place sts on smooth waste yarn or holder.

SLEEVES

With MC and smaller needles, CO 88 sts. Work in k2, p2 rib for 2 rows and *at the same time* dec 1 st on the last (WS) row—87 sts rem. Change to larger straight needles. *Next row:* (RS) K1 (selvedge st), work Row 1 of Sleeve chart across 85 sts, k1 (selvedge st). Keeping the first and last st of every row in St st, cont as established through Row 13 of chart. Change to MC. *Next row:* (WS) P10 (10, 15, 15), [pm, p11 (11, 14, 14)] 7 (7, 4, 4) times, [pm, p0 (0, 16, 16)] 0 (0, 1, 1) time. *Dec row 1:* (RS) [Knit to m, slip marker (sl m), sl 1, k1, psso] 7 (7, 5, 5) times, knit to end—80 (80, 82, 82) sts rem. Work even for 5 rows. *Dec row 2:* (RS) [Knit to 2 sts before m, k2tog, sl m] 7 (7, 5, 5) times, knit to end—73 (73, 77, 77) sts rem. Work even for 5 rows. Rep dec row 1—66 (66, 72, 72) sts rem. *Next row:* (WS) Purl, dec 0 (0, 2, 2) sts evenly spaced and removing markers when you come to them—66 (66, 70, 70) sts rem. Change to smaller needles. *Next row:* (RS) K2, *p2, k2; rep from *. Cont in k2, p2 rib as established until ribbed section measures 4 (4, 5, 6)" (10 [10, 12.5, 15] cm), ending with a WS row.

Shape Armhole

Cont in rib, BO 4 sts at beg of next 2 rows, then BO 1 st at beg of foll 4 (6, 8, 8) rows—54 (52, 54, 54) sts rem. Place sts on holder.

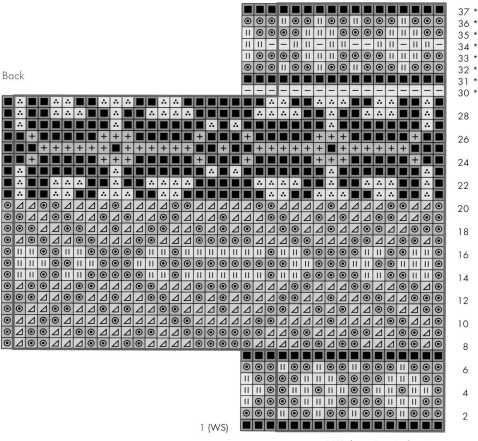

Back

1 (WS)

37 *
36 *
35 *
34 *
33 *
32 *
31 *
30 *

28

26

24

22

20

18

16

14

12

10

8

6

4

2

* Work as given in directions

Work the same patterns
in different colors for the
front and back.

Front

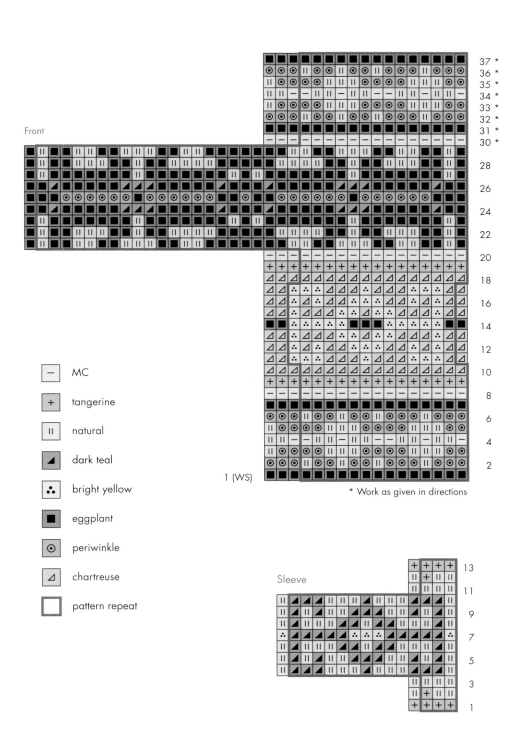

37 *
36 *
35 *
34 *
33 *
32 *
31 *
30 *
28
26
24
22
20
18
16
14
12
10
8
6
4
2

1 (WS)

* Work as given in directions

—	MC
+	tangerine
‖	natural
◢	dark teal
∴	bright yellow
■	eggplant
⊙	periwinkle
◿	chartreuse
☐	pattern repeat

Sleeve

13
11
9
7
5
3
1

YOKE

Place one set of 54 (52, 54, 54) sleeve sts on each side of cir needle holding 54 (60, 66, 74) back sts—162 (164, 174, 182) sts total. The yoke will be worked in two sections; the back plus one-half of each sleeve and the front plus the other half of each sleeve. The two sections will be seamed during the finishing.

Back Half

With MC, RS facing, and beg at one sleeve, k10 (7, 4, 0), work 17 (19, 23, 27) sts in rib as established to center of sleeve, then slip the 27 (26, 27, 27) sts just worked onto holder, use the backward-loop method (see Glossary, page 133) to CO 1 st (for selvedge st at center of sleeve), work 17 (19, 23, 27) sts in rib as established, k10 (7, 4, 0) to end of sleeve, k26 (29, 32, 36) back sts, k2tog, k26 (29, 32, 36) rem sts of back, work other sleeve as foll: k10 (7, 4, 0), work 17 (19, 23, 27) sts in rib as established to center of sleeve, use the backward-loop method to CO 1 st (for selvedge st at center of sleeve), then slip rem 27 (26, 27, 27) sleeve sts to a holder. *Note:* The yoke is shaped at the same time as the shoulders; read all the way through the foll section before proceeding. Cont on 109 (113, 121, 129) sts as foll:

Row 1: (WS) With MC, p1 (selvedge st), work 17 (19, 23, 27) sts in rib as established, pm, work Row 1 of Back chart across 73 sts, pm, join a second ball of MC and work 17 (19, 23, 27) sts in rib as established, p1 (selvedge st).

Row 2: (RS) With MC, k2, p2tog (for shoulder dec), rib to m, sl m, work Row 2 of chart to next m, sl m, rib to last 4 sts, p2tog (for shoulder dec), k1, sl 1—2 sts dec'd.

Cont as established, working WS rows as p2, k1 at beg of row and k1, p1, sl 1 at end of row and *at the same time* rep shoulder dec at each shoulder edge every 4th row 4 (3, 0, 0) more times, then every other row 9 (11, 17, 17) times and also *at the same time* shape charted section between m as foll:

Chart Row 30: Work to m, sl m, ssk, k2, k2tog, [k7, k2tog] 7 times, k2, k2tog, sl m, work to end—63 sts rem between markers.

Chart Rows 31, 33, and 35: Work to m, sl m, p2tog, purl to 2 sts before m, ssp (see Glossary, page 134), sl m, work to end—2 sts dec'd between markers each row; 53 sts rem between markers after Row 35.

Chart Rows 32, 34, and 36: Work to m, sl m, ssk, knit to 2 sts before m, k2tog, sl m, work to end—2 sts dec'd between markers each row; 51 sts rem between markers after Row 36.

Chart Row 37: Work to m, sl m, p2tog, p1, p3tog, [p4, p3tog] 6 times, p1, ssp, sl m, work to end—43 (45, 47, 55) sts rem total; 35 sts rem between markers.

Place sts on holder.

Front Plus Half Sleeves

Place 54 (60, 66, 74) front sts onto cir needle, then place 27 (26, 27, 27) sts of each sleeve onto cir needle so that one sleeve is on each side of the front sts—108 (112, 120, 128) sts total. Work as for back, substituting Front chart for Back chart, through Row 30 of chart—77 (79, 81, 89) sts rem; yoke measures 6¼" (16 cm) from joining row.

Shape Front Neck

(WS; chart Row 31) Cont in patt, work to m, p2tog, work 24 (24, 23, 22) sts, BO center 11 (11, 13, 15) sts with MC, work in patt to 2 sts before m, ssp, work to end—32 (33, 33, 36) sts rem each side. Working each side separately, cont working shoulder decs as for back and *at the same time* dec 1 st after first m and before second m every row 6 times and also *at the same time* BO 3 (3, 3, 5) sts at each neck edge 3 (3, 3, 1) time(s), then BO 4 sts at each neck edge 0 (0, 0, 2) times—14 (15, 15, 14) sts rem each side.

FINISHING

Weave in loose ends.

Neckband

With MC, cir needle, RS facing, and beg at left front neck sts, k2tog, k12 (13, 13, 12), pick up and knit 11 (11, 13, 15) sts across center neck, k12 (13, 13, 12) right front neck sts, ssk, work across 43 (45, 47, 55) back neck sts as foll: k2tog, k12 (12, 13, 16), k2tog, k11 (13, 13, 15), k2tog, k12 (12, 13, 16), ssk—76 (80, 84, 92) sts total. Work in k2, p2 rib until piece measures 1½" (3.8 cm) from pick-up rnd. *Next rnd:* [K2, p2, k2, k3tog, sl 1, k2tog, psso] 3 times, [k2, p2] 4 (5, 5, 6) times, k2, k3tog, sl 1, k2tog, psso, [k2, p2] 4 (4, 5, 6) times—60 (64, 68, 76) sts rem. Work in k2, p2 rib until piece measures 2½" [6.5 cm] from pick-up rnd. BO all sts.

With MC threaded on a tapestry needle, sew upper sleeve and shoulder seams. Sew upper sleeves to body at armholes. Sew side and sleeve seams. Block lightly.

FAUX-EMBROIDERY YOKE SWEATER
ROBIN MELANSON

Robin Melanson drew upon several knitting traditions in this round-yoke pullover that mimics the silhouette and style of classic Swedish Bohus Strickning garments. In addition to bands of Fair Isle color stranding, she worked floats of contrasting colors, then caught the floats into stitches a few rows later to give the look of embroidery. She also added two-color raised Latvian braids around the keyhole neck (which can be worn at the front or back), cuffs, and lower body. Not only does the braid provide visual interest, it also works to keep the edges from rolling—there's no need for ribbing. This pullover is worked in the round from the neck down, with the shaping increases limited to solid-color areas where they don't interrupt the color patterning.

NOTES

✦ The sweater is worked from the neck down.

✦ The yoke is worked back and forth until the keyhole is completed, then joined, and the remaining body is worked in the round to the lower edge.

STITCH GUIDE

Latvian Braid in Rows (mult of 2 sts + 1)

Row 1: (RS) *K1 with CC4, k1 with CC1; rep from * to last st, k1 with CC4.

Row 2: (WS) Holding yarns at back of work, k1 with CC4, *bring CC1 over CC4 and k1 with CC1, bring CC4 over CC1 and k1 with CC4; rep from * to end (the yarns will be twisted after this row, but will untwist on next row).

Row 3: (RS) Holding yarns at front of work, p1 with CC4, *bring CC1 over CC4 and p1 with CC1, bring CC4 over CC1 and p1 with CC4; rep from * to end.

Latvian Braid in Rounds (mult of 2 sts)

Rnd 1: *K1 with CC4, k1 with CC1; rep from * to end.

Rnd 2: Holding yarns at front of work, p1 with CC4, *bring CC1 under CC4 and p1 with CC1, bring CC4 under CC1 and p1 with CC4; rep from * to end (the yarns will be twisted after this rnd, but will untwist on next rnd).

Rnd 3: Holding yarns at front of work, p1 with CC4, *bring CC1 over CC4 and p1 with CC1, bring CC4 over CC1 and p1 with CC4; rep from * to end.

FINISHED SIZE
32¾ (35¼, 38¾, 42½, 46, 49¼)" (83 [89.5, 98.5, 108, 117, 125] cm) bust circumference. Sweater shown measures 35¼" (89.5 cm).

YARN
Worsted weight (#4 Medium).

Shown here: Classic Elite Inca Alpaca (100% alpaca; 109 yd [100 m]/50 g): #1176 gaucho grey heather (light yellow-gray heather; MC), 7 (7, 8, 9, 10, 11) skeins; #1120 Kentucky teal (blue-green heather; CC1), #1198 persimmon (burnt orange; CC2), #1142 Cajamaica maroon (red-purple heather; CC3), #1108 lamas heather (dark purple heather; CC4), 1 skein each.

NEEDLES
Body—size U.S. 7 (4.5 mm): 24" and 32" (60 and 80 cm) circular (cir). Sleeves—size U.S. 7 (4.5 mm): set of 4 or 5 double-pointed (dpn). Adjust needle size if necessary to obtain the correct gauge.

NOTIONS
Markers (m); waste yarn; tapestry needle; one ⅜" (1 cm) button.

GAUGE
20 stitches and 24 rounds = 4" (10 cm) in stockinette stitch, worked in rounds.

FAUX EMBROIDERY

On the float rows (right side), pass the contrasting yarn back and forth between the right and wrong sides of the work according to the charted pattern while knitting with the main color (Figure 1), anchoring long floats on the wrong side in the same manner used to catch long floats in Fair Isle knitting. Two rows later, catch the float with a stitch by lifting the float with the right needle and working it together with the stitch on the needle (Figure 2).

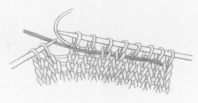

Figure 1

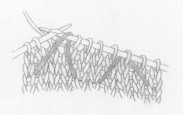

Figure 2

YOKE

With MC and shorter cir needle, CO 81 (85, 89, 93, 97, 101) sts. Do not join. Knit 1 (WS) row. Work Rows 1–3 of Latvian braid in rows (see Stitch Guide). *Next row:* (WS) Change to MC and purl, inc 4 (6, 8, 10, 12, 14) sts evenly spaced—85 (91, 97, 103, 109, 115) sts. Work Row 5 (4, 3, 3, 2, 1) of Yoke chart 28 (30, 32, 34, 36, 38) times, place marker (pm), k1. *Note:* Row numbers will not always be odd on RS rows and even on WS rows due to row omissions for different sizes. Cont working 84 (90, 96, 102, 108, 114) sts as charted and 1 st in St st through Row 12 of chart, omitting indicated rows for your size and inc 28 (30, 32, 34, 36, 38) sts as indicated on Row 6—113 (121, 129, 137, 145, 153) sts. *Joining row:* (RS; Row 13 of chart) Work as charted to last 2 sts, k2tog with MC, pm, and join for working in rnds—112 (120, 128, 136, 144, 152) sts rem. Cont through Rnd 59 of chart, omitting indicated rnds for your size, changing to longer cir needle when necessary, and ending Rnds 27, 30, 33, 36, 39, and 42 one st before end-of-rnd marker, then beg Rnds 28, 31, 34, 37, 40, and 43 with last st of previous rnd to ensure that floats can be completed over required number of sts without a jog—252 (270, 288, 306, 324, 342) sts; piece measures about 7½ (7¾, 8¼, 8¾, 9½, 10½)" (19 [19.5, 21, 22, 24, 26.5] cm) from CO.

Floats of contrasting yarn that are caught in stitches on subsequent rows give the look of embroidery, but without the fuss.

Yoke

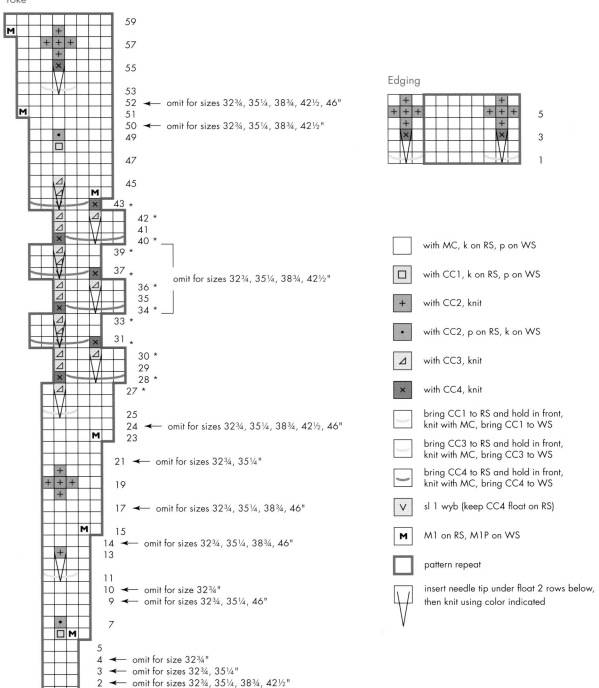

59

57

M 55

53
52 ← omit for sizes 32¾, 35¼, 38¾, 42½, 46"
51
M 50 ← omit for sizes 32¾, 35¼, 38¾, 42½"
49

47

45

43 *
42 *
41
40 * ⎫
39 * ⎬ omit for sizes 32¾, 35¼, 38¾, 42½"
37 *
36 * ⎬
35
34 * ⎭
33 *
31 *
30 *
29
28 *
27 *

25
24 ← omit for sizes 32¾, 35¼, 38¾, 42½, 46"
23

21 ← omit for sizes 32¾, 35¼"

19

17 ← omit for sizes 32¾, 35¼, 38¾, 46"

M 15
14 ← omit for sizes 32¾, 35¼, 38¾, 46"
13

11
10 ← omit for size 32¾"
9 ← omit for sizes 32¾, 35¼, 46"

7

5
4 ← omit for size 32¾"
3 ← omit for sizes 32¾, 35¼"
2 ← omit for sizes 32¾, 35¼, 38¾, 42½"
1 ← omit for sizes 32¾, 35¼, 38¾, 42½, 46"

* Work as given in directions

Edging

5

3

1

☐ with MC, k on RS, p on WS

▢ with CC1, k on RS, p on WS

✚ with CC2, knit

• with CC2, p on RS, k on WS

◿ with CC3, knit

✕ with CC4, knit

bring CC1 to RS and hold in front,
knit with MC, bring CC1 to WS

bring CC3 to RS and hold in front,
knit with MC, bring CC3 to WS

bring CC4 to RS and hold in front,
knit with MC, bring CC4 to WS

V sl 1 wyb (keep CC4 float on RS)

M M1 on RS, M1P on WS

☐ pattern repeat

insert needle tip under float 2 rows below,
then knit using color indicated

Use knitted-in braids
to form colorful
accents that prevent
edges from rolling.

BODY

Cont with MC only, k36 (39, 43, 46, 50, 53), place next 53 (56, 58, 60, 62, 65) sts on waste yarn for sleeve, use the backward-loop method (see Glossary, page 133) to CO 9 (9, 11, 13, 15, 17) sts over gap, k73 (79, 86, 93, 100, 106), place next 53 (56, 58, 60, 62, 65) sts on waste yarn for other sleeve, CO 9 (9, 11, 13, 15, 17) sts over gap as before, k37 (40, 43, 47, 50, 53), remove marker, knit to center underarm st, pm on each side of center underarm st; first marker denotes new beg of rnd—164 (176, 194, 212, 230, 246) sts total. Place additional markers on each side of center st on opposite armhole. Work 4 rnds even. *Dec rnd:* K1 (marked st), k2tog, knit to 2 sts before marked st on opposite underarm, ssk, k1 (marked st), k2tog, knit to last 2 sts, ssk—4 sts dec'd. Work 6 rnds even. Rep last 7 rnds 6 more times—136 (148, 166, 184, 202, 218) sts rem. *Inc rnd:* K1, sl m, M1L (see Glossary, page 137), knit to next m, M1R (see Glossary, page 137), sl m, k1, sl m, M1L, knit to end of rnd, M1R, sl m—4 sts inc'd. Inc 4 sts in this manner every 4th rnd 3 (3, 3, 3, 0, 0) more times, then every 5th rnd 0 (0, 1, 1, 4, 4) time(s)—152 (164, 186, 204, 222, 238) sts. Work 3 (3, 1, 1, 1, 1) rnd(s) even—piece measures about 11¾ (11¾, 12¼, 12¼, 12¾, 12¾)" (30 [30, 31, 31, 32.5, 32.5] cm) from underarm CO sts. *Next rnd:* (inc for sizes 32¾" and 35¼" only) *K1, sl m, M1L 1 (1, 0, 0, 0, 0) time, k4 (3, 4, 1, 1, 1), pm, rep first 8 sts of Rnd 1 of Edging chart 8 (9, 10, 12, 13, 14) times, work last 3 sts of chart, pm, k4 (3, 5, 1, 2, 2), M1R 1 (1, 0, 0, 0, 0) time, sl m; rep from * to end—156 (168, 186, 204, 222, 238) sts. Cont working chart as established through Rnd 6 and *at the same time* rep inc rnd on Rnd 5 (5, 3, 3, 3, 3) of chart—160 (172, 190, 208, 226, 242) sts. Cont with MC only, work 2 (2, 1, 1, 1, 1) rnd(s) even, then rep inc rnd once more—164 (176, 194, 212, 230, 246) sts. Work 0 (0, 1, 1, 1, 1) rnd even in MC. Work Rnds 1–3 of Latvian braid in rnds (see Stitch Guide). With MC, knit 1 rnd. Loosely BO all sts pwise.

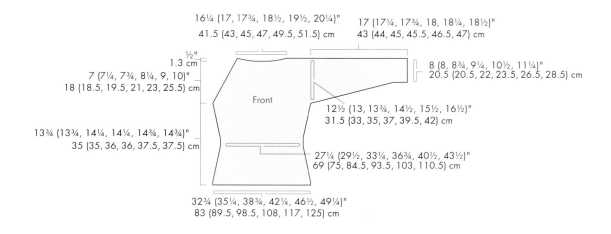

16¼ (17, 17¾, 18½, 19½, 20¼)"
41.5 (43, 45, 47, 49.5, 51.5) cm

17 (17¼, 17¾, 18, 18¼, 18½)"
43 (44, 45, 45.5, 46.5, 47) cm

½"
1.3 cm

7 (7¼, 7¾, 8¼, 9, 10)"
18 (18.5, 19.5, 21, 23, 25.5) cm

8 (8, 8¾, 9¼, 10½, 11¼)"
20.5 (20.5, 22, 23.5, 26.5, 28.5) cm

Front

12½ (13, 13¾, 14½, 15½, 16½)"
31.5 (33, 35, 37, 39.5, 42) cm

13¾ (13¾, 14¼, 14¼, 14¾, 14¾)"
35 (35, 36, 36, 37.5, 37.5) cm

27¼ (29½, 33¼, 36¾, 40½, 43½)"
69 (75, 84.5, 93.5, 103, 110.5) cm

32¾ (35¼, 38¾, 42¼, 46½, 49¼)"
83 (89.5, 98.5, 108, 117, 125) cm

SLEEVES

Divide 53 (56, 58, 60, 62, 65) held sleeve sts evenly onto 3 or 4 dpn. Rejoin MC and pick up and knit 9 (9, 11, 13, 15, 17) sts at base of underarm CO sts of body, pm on each side of center underarm st (first marker denotes beg of rnd), k53 (56, 58, 60, 62, 65) sleeve sts, join for working in rnds, knit to m—62 (65, 69, 73, 77, 82) sts total. Work 3 rnds even. *Dec rnd:* K1 (marked st), k2tog, knit to last 2 sts, ssk—2 sts dec'd. Rep dec rnd every 9th rnd 4 (0, 1, 2, 4, 0) more time(s), then every 8th rnd 6 (9, 10, 9, 7, 10) times, then every 7th rnd 0 (2, 0, 0, 0, 2) times—40 (41, 45, 49, 53, 56) sts rem. Work even if necessary until sleeve measures 15 (15¼, 15¾, 16, 16¼, 16½)" (38 [38.5, 40, 40.5, 41.5, 42] cm) from pick-up rnd. *Next rnd:* K3 (3, 1, 3, 1, 3), pm, rep first 8 sts of Rnd 1 of Edging chart 4 (4, 5, 5, 6, 6) times, work last 3 sts of chart, pm, k2 (3, 1, 3, 1, 2). Cont as established through Rnd 6 of chart—piece measures 16 (16¼, 16¾, 17, 17¼, 17½)" (40.5 [41.5, 42.5, 43, 44, 44.5] cm) from underarm pick-up. With MC, knit 3 rnds, dec 0 (1, 1, 1, 1, 0) st on last rnd—40 (40, 44, 48, 52, 56) sts rem. Work Rnds 1–3 of Latvian braid in rnds. With MC, knit 1 rnd. Loosely BO all sts pwise.

FINISHING

Block garment to measurements. Weave in loose ends, paying close attention to the underarms. With MC threaded on a tapestry needle, work closely spaced blanket sts (see Glossary, page 135) around keyhole opening, forming a button loop on the left side of the keyhole by making a loop of yarn at upper corner, taking a stitch to secure it, then working blanket sts over it. Sew button to right side of keyhole, opposite button loop.

Deborah Newton united stockinette-stitch stripes, contrasting garter ridges, and a simple honeycomb slip-stitch pattern for the colorful pattern play on the cuffs and yoke of this turtleneck pullover. The body is worked in the round to the armholes, as are the sleeves. They are then joined, and the yoke is worked in a single piece to the high foldover turtleneck, which ends with a few bright stripes. The sleeves begin with a strip of the color-work pattern used for the yoke. For the cuff, stitches are picked up along one selvedge edge and worked for a few rounds in single rib. For the top portion of the sleeve, more stitches are picked up along the other selvedge edge and worked in stockinette stitch to the armholes.

CUFF (MAKE 2)

With blue and larger needle, CO 36 sts. Do not join. Working the first and last st in garter st (knit every row) throughout, work center 34 sts as foll: Work 4 (4, 6, 6) rows in St st (knit RS rows; purl WS rows), ending with a WS row. Beg and end as indicated for cuff, work Rows 1–20 of Honeycomb chart, using green for CC1, wine for CC2, blue for CC3, and orange for CC4. With wine, work 4 (4, 6, 6) rows in St st. Beg and end as indicated for cuff, work Rows 1–20 of chart again, using gold for CC1, blue for CC2, wine for CC3, and green for CC4. With blue, work 4 (4, 6, 6) rows in St st. Beg and end as indicated for cuff, work Rows 1–20 of chart again, using orange for CC1, wine for CC2, blue for CC3, and gold for CC4. With wine, work 4 (4, 6, 6) rows in St st. With gold, knit 2 rows. With blue, work 4 (4, 6, 6) rows in St st. With green, knit 2 rows. With wine, work 4 (4, 6, 6) rows in St st. With orange, knit 2 rows—piece measures about 9 (9, 10¾, 10¾)" (23 [23, 27.5, 27.5] cm) from CO. BO all sts. Weave in loose ends. Steam very lightly.

Edging

With wine, smaller needle, and RS facing, pick up and knit 63 (63, 75, 75) sts evenly spaced along one long side of one cuff for one sleeve, and along the other long side of the other cuff for the other sleeve. Work in k1, p1 rib for 3 rows. BO all sts in patt. With wine threaded on a tapestry needle, sew CO end of cuff to BO end.

FINISHED SIZE
36 (40, 44, 48)" (91.5 [101.5, 112, 122] cm) bust circumference. Sweater shown measures 36" (91.5 cm).

YARN
Sportweight (#2 Fine).

Shown here: Reynolds Whiskey (100% wool; 195 yd [178 m]/50 g): #016 wine, 6 (7, 8, 8) balls; #053 blue, #101 gold, #102 orange, and #103 green, 1 ball each.

NEEDLES
Body and sleeves—size U.S. 7 (4.5 mm): 16" and 24" (40 and 60 cm) circular (cir) and set of 4 or 5 double-pointed (dpn). Edging—size U.S. 5 (3.75 mm): 24" (60 cm) cir. Adjust needle size if necessary to obtain the correct gauge.

NOTIONS
Markers (m); stitch holders; tapestry needle.

GAUGE
22 stitches and 28 rounds = 4" (10 cm) in stockinette stitch on larger needle, worked in rounds.

SLEEVES

Fold seamed cuff along the center of the second slip-st band (wine stripe between 2 gold ridges), and with cuff folded flat, mark the opposite fold on the non-ribbed edge to denote beg of rnd. With wine, dpn, RS facing, and beg at marker, pick up and knit 58 (58, 70, 70) sts evenly spaced around cuff. Divide sts evenly among 3 or 4 dpn and join for working in rnds. Place marker (pm) after first st of rnd and before last st of rnd. Work even in St st (knit every rnd) until piece measures 1½" (3.8 cm) from pick-up rnd. *Inc rnd:* K1, slip marker (sl m), M1 (see Glossary, page 137), knit to next m, M1, sl m, k1—2 sts inc'd. Cont in St st, rep inc rnd every 2 (1, 1½, 1)" (5 [2.5, 3.8, 2.5] cm) 4 (9, 7, 10) more times—68 (78, 86, 92) sts. Work even until piece measures 18¼ (19, 19½, 20½)" (46.5 [48.5, 49.5, 52] cm) from lower edge of ribbing on cuff. *Next rnd:* BO 6 sts, knit to last 6 sts, BO to end—56 (66, 74, 80) sts rem. Cut yarn and place sts on holder.

Work two-row garter stripes to add colorful relief to stockinette stitch.

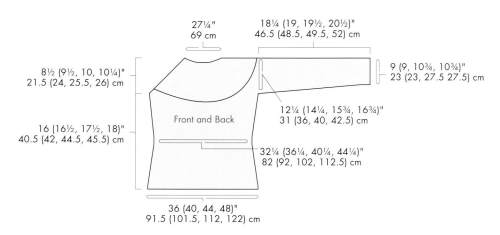

27¼"
69 cm

18¼ (19, 19½, 20½)"
46.5 (48.5, 49.5, 52) cm

8½ (9½, 10, 10¼)"
21.5 (24, 25.5, 26) cm

9 (9, 10¾, 10¾)"
23 (23, 27.5 27.5) cm

Front and Back

12¼ (14¼, 15¾, 16¾)"
31 (36, 40, 42.5) cm

16 (16½, 17½, 18)"
40.5 (42, 44.5, 45.5) cm

32¼ (36¼, 40¼, 44¼)"
82 (92, 102, 112.5) cm

36 (40, 44, 48)"
91.5 (101.5, 112, 122) cm

BODY

With wine and smaller cir needle, CO 218 (242, 266, 290) sts. Pm and join for working in rnds, being careful not to twist sts. Rnd begins at side "seam." Work in k1, p1 rib until piece measures 1" (2.5 cm) from CO and *at the same time* dec 20 (22, 24, 26) sts evenly spaced on last rnd—198 (220, 242, 264) sts rem. Change to larger cir needle. Place additional marker after 99 (110, 121, 132) sts to mark other side "seam"—99 (110, 121, 132) sts each for front and back. Place additional markers 2 sts before and 2 sts after each "seam" marker—6 markers total. Work even in St st for 10 (12, 16, 18) rnds. *Dec rnd:* *K2, sl m, ssk, work to 2 sts before next m, k2tog, sl m, k2, sl m; rep from * once—4 sts dec'd. Rep dec rnd every 8th rnd 4 more times—178 (200, 222, 244) sts rem. Work even until piece measures 10 (10½, 11½, 12)" (25.5 [26.5, 29, 30.5] cm) from CO. *Inc rnd:* *K2, sl m, M1, work to next m, M1, sl m, k2, sl m; rep from * once—4 sts inc'd. Rep inc rnd every 8th rnd 4 more times—198 (220, 242, 264) sts. Work even until piece measures 16 (16½, 17½, 18)" (40.5 [42, 44.5, 45.5] cm) from CO.

Divide for Front and Back

Removing markers as you come to them, BO 6 sts, knit to 6 sts before side m, BO 12 sts, knit to last 6 sts, BO to end—87 (98, 109, 120) sts rem each for front and back. Cut yarn.

Honeycomb

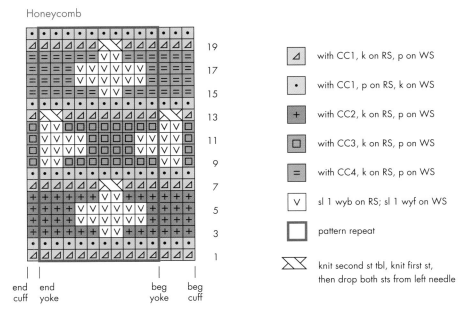

◢	with CC1, k on RS, p on WS
•	with CC1, p on RS, k on WS
+	with CC2, k on RS, p on WS
□	with CC3, k on RS, p on WS
=	with CC4, k on RS, p on WS
V	sl 1 wyb on RS; sl 1 wyf on WS
⬜	pattern repeat
⋈	knit second st tbl, knit first st, then drop both sts from left needle

Mix stripes and slip-stitch patterns to produce a colorful honeycomb pattern.

YOKE

With wine and larger longer cir needle, k87 (98, 109, 120) back sts, pm, k56 (66, 74, 80) left sleeve sts, pm, k87 (98, 109, 120) front sts, pm, k56 (66, 74, 80) right sleeve sts—286 (328, 366, 400) sts total. Pm and join for working in rnds. With wine, knit 5 (8, 11, 9) rnds. With orange, knit 1 rnd, then purl 1 rnd. With blue, knit 4 (5, 5, 6) rnds and *at the same time* inc 4 (2, 4, 0) sts on last rnd—290 (330, 370, 400) sts. If desired, remove all but end-of-rnd marker. Beg and end as indicated for yoke, work Rnds 1–20 of Honeycomb chart, using green for CC1, wine for CC2, blue for CC3, and orange for CC4.

With wine, knit 4 (5, 5, 6) rnds and *at the same time* dec 40 (60, 70, 80) sts evenly spaced on last rnd—250 (270, 300, 320) sts rem. Beg and end as indicated for yoke, work Rnds 1–20 of Honeycomb chart, using gold for CC1, blue for CC2, wine for CC3, and green for CC4. With blue, knit 4 (5, 5, 6) rnds and *at the same time* dec 50 (60, 70, 80) sts evenly spaced on last rnd—200 (210, 230, 240) sts rem. Beg and end as indicated for yoke, work Rnds 1–20 of Honeycomb chart, using orange for CC1, wine for CC2, blue for CC3, and gold for CC4. With wine, knit 4 (5, 5, 6) rnds and *at the same time* dec 50 (60, 80, 90) sts evenly spaced on last rnd—150 sts rem. With green, knit 1 rnd, then purl 1 rnd.

Shape Neck

With wine, k50, pm, knit to end of rnd.
Work short-rows (see Glossary, page 139)
as foll: Knit to 5 sts beyond m, wrap next st,
turn work, purl to 5 sts beyond beg-of-rnd m,
wrap next st, turn. Working wraps tog with
wrapped sts when you come to them, *work
4 sts beyond last wrapped st, wrap next st,
turn; rep from * 5 more times—20 sts worked
after each marker. Turn work and work
across all sts to end of rnd—still 150 sts.

Collar

With wine, knit 1 rnd, dec 2 sts evenly
spaced—148 sts rem. Work even in k2,
p2 rib until ribbed section measures 9"
(23 cm). Cont in rib, work 3 rnds each of
green, wine, orange, wine, and gold.
With blue, work in rib for 1" (2.5 cm).
Loosely BO all sts.

FINISHING

Weave in loose ends. With wine threaded
on a tapestry needle, sew underarm seams.
Block lightly to measurements.

In the fine tradition of Bohus-style colorwork, **Chrissy Gardiner** decorated her knee-highs with colorful cuffs that include both knit and purl stitches in an intricate pattern that's actually quite easy to knit. She worked the legs and insteps in an elastic knit-two-purl-two ribbing and shaped the backs of the legs with decreases for a comfortable fit, no matter the shape of your legs. The socks are worked in rounds from the cast-on at the top of the leg to the Kitchener stitch at the tip of the toes. Chrissy added blocks of color at the heel and stripes at the toe for a playful contrast to the socks' sober gray.

FINISHED SIZE
About 7½" (19 cm) foot circumference, 12" (30.5 cm) calf circumference, and 8½" (21.5 cm) foot length.

YARN
Fingering weight (#1 Super Fine).
Shown here: Classic Elite Alpaca Sox (60% alpaca, 20% merino, 20% nylon; 450 yd [411 m]/100 g): #1803 ash (light gray; MC), #1848 sky (light blue; CC1), #1855 russet (rust; CC2), and #1881 granny smith (green; CC3), 1 skein each.

NEEDLES
Size U.S. 1 (2.25 mm): set of 5 double-pointed (dpn). Adjust needle size if necessary to obtain the correct gauge.

NOTIONS
Marker (m); tapestry needle.

GAUGE
17 stitches and 23 rounds = 2" (5 cm) in stockinette stitch worked in rounds.

> **NOTE**
> ✤ If your calf is very slender (less than 14" [35.5 cm] around), you may want to work the charted color pattern on one size smaller needles.

CUFF

With CC1, CO 104 sts. Arrange sts so there are 16 sts on each of Needles 1 and 2 (front of leg and instep sts) and 36 sts on each of Needles 3 and 4 (back of leg and heel sts). Place marker (pm) and join for working in rnds, being careful not to twist sts. Rnd begins at side of leg. *Set-up rnd:* K1, *p2, k2; rep from * to last 3 sts, p2, k1. Cut off CC1. Join MC and cont in rib as established until piece measures 1" (2.5 cm) from CO.

LEG

Joining and cutting off colors as necessary, work Rnds 1–37 of Bohus chart across all sts, purling sts as specified. Rejoin MC and work rib as before for 3 rnds. *Dec rnd:* Work rib as established to last 2 sts of Needle 3, k2tog, ssk, work rib as established to end of rnd—2 sts dec'd. Work rib as established for 3 rnds, then rep dec rnd—100 sts rem. Work rib as established for 1 rnd, then rep dec rnd. Rep the last 2 rnds 11 more times—76 sts rem. Work rib as established for 3 rnds, then rep dec rnd. Rep the last 4 rnds 5 more times—64 sts rem. Cont in rib as established until piece measures 14" (35.5 cm) from CO, or desired length to top of heel, ending with Needle 2. Cut off MC.

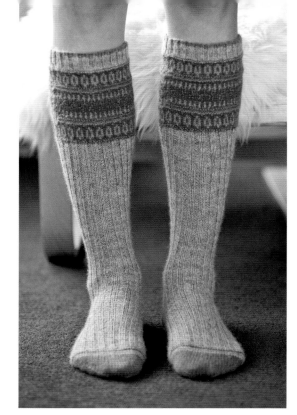
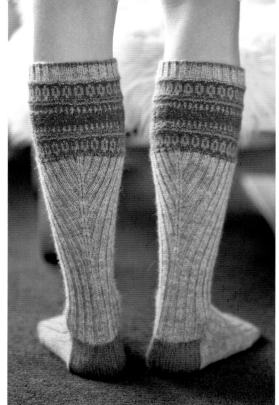

Purl selected stitches to add texture to a Fair Isle pattern.

HEEL

Join CC1 and knit all sts on Needles 3 and 4 onto a single needle—32 heel sts; rem 32 sts will be worked later for instep.

Heel Flap

Work 32 heel sts back and forth in rows as foll:

Row 1: (WS) Sl 1 purlwise with yarn in front (pwise wyf), purl to end.

Row 2: *Sl 1 purlwise with yarn in back (pwise wyb), k1; rep from * to end.

Rep these 2 rows 15 more times, then work Row 1 once more—16 chain sts along right selvedge edge and 17 chain sts along left selvedge edge.

Turn Heel

Work short-rows to shape heel as foll:

Row 1: (RS) Sl 1 pwise wyb, k16, ssk, k1, turn work.

Row 2: Sl 1 pwise wyf, p3, p2tog, p1, turn.

Row 3: Sl 1 pwise wyb, knit to 1 st before gap formed on previous row, ssk (1 st each side of gap), k1, turn.

Row 4: Sl 1 pwise wyf, purl to 1 st before gap formed on previous row, p2tog (1 st each side of gap), p1, turn.

Rep Rows 3 and 4 five more times—18 heel sts rem. Cut off CC1.

Shape Gusset

Pick up sts along selvedge edge of heel flap and rejoin for working in rnds as foll: Join MC and knit across heel sts, dividing them so that there are 9 sts each on Needles 3 and 4. Cont with Needle 4, pick up and knit 18 sts along the selvedge edge of the heel flap. Work rib as established across Needles 1 and 2. With an empty needle, pick up and knit 18 sts along other selvedge edge of heel flap, then k9 sts on Needle 3—86 sts total. With an empty needle, knit to the last 3 sts on Needle 4, k2tog, k1—85 sts rem; 16 sts each on Needles 1 and 2 (instep), 27 sts on Needle 3, and 26 sts on Needle 4. Rejoin for working in rnds.

Rnd 1: Needles 1 and 2: work in rib as established; Needle 3: k1, ssk, knit to end; Needle 4: knit—1 st dec'd.

Rnd 2: Needles 1 and 2: work in rib as established; Needle 3: knit; Needle 4: knit to last 3 sts, k2tog, k1—1 st dec'd.

Rep these 2 rnds 9 more times, then work Rnd 1 once more—64 sts rem; 16 sts on each needle.

FOOT

Cont working established rib on Needles 1 and 2 (instep) and St st on Needles 3 and 4 (sole) until piece measures about 6" (15 cm) from back of heel, or about 2½" (6.5 cm) less than desired total length. Knit 1 rnd across all sts. Knit 1 rnd each with CC2, MC, CC3, then MC. Cut off all colors.

TOE

Join CC1 and dec as foll:

Rnd 1: Needle 1: k1, ssk, knit to end; Needle 2: knit to last 3 sts, k2tog, k1; Needle 3: k1, ssk, knit to end; Needle 4: knit to last 3 sts, k2tog, k1—4 sts dec'd.

Rnd 2: Knit.

Rep Rnds 1 and 2 seven more times—32 sts rem. Rep Rnd 1 only (dec every rnd) 4 times—16 sts rem. Sl 4 sts from Needle 2 onto Needle 1, then sl 4 sts from Needle 4 onto Needle 3—8 sts each on 2 needles. Cut yarn, leaving a 12" (30.5 cm) tail.

FINISHING

Thread tail on a tapestry needle and use the Kitchener st (see Glossary, page 136) to graft the rem sts tog. Weave in loose ends. Dampen socks and lay flat or place on sock blockers to dry.

Bohus

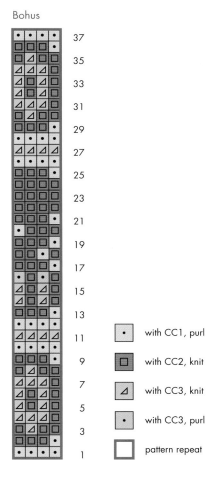

•	with CC1, purl
▢	with CC2, knit
◿	with CC3, knit
•	with CC3, purl
☐	pattern repeat

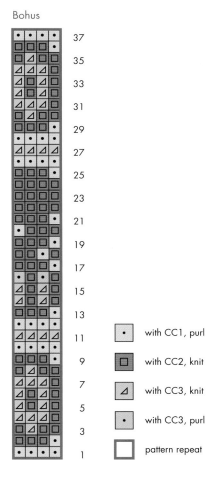

HARVEST CARDIGAN
ROBIN MELANSON

When she was choosing a palette for her Fair Isle cardigan, **Robin Melanson** turned to two seemingly unrelated sources—the colorful seed heads and foliage of wild grasses and the cover of Neil Young's 1972 album *Harvest*—for inspiration. She worked the body in rounds, using steeks at the front opening and armholes so that she looked only at the right side of the piece as she knitted. For simplicity, Robin maintained the same background color throughout, but she shaded the pattern colors rhythmically from dark to light then back to dark. For added texture, she purled selected stitches in the Bohus tradition and added embroidered details as a nod to the flower-child styles of the 1970s. The colorful ribbing at the hem, cuffs, and neck is worked in a corrugated rib that stabilizes the stitches without drawing them together.

NOTES

✦ The body is knitted in the round from the lower edge to the neck, with steeks at the center front and armholes. After the knitting is completed, the steeks are secured with machine-stitching and cut open.

✦ The sleeves are knitted in the round to the underarm, then the caps are worked back and forth in rows.

✦ On the Body chart, sizes 37" (green line) and 46¼" (purple line) share the same shaping line; only the 46¼" line is visible. On these rounds, follow the 46¼" line for both sizes.

✦ On the Sleeve chart, sizes 35" (brown line) and 49¾" (light blue line) share the same shaping line; only the 35" line is visible. Follow the 35" line for both sizes.

✦ The beginning of the round is at the left underarm (unlike many cardigans, where the beginning of the round is at the center front edge) to allow for the option of making a pullover.

✦ To adjust the pattern for a pullover, simply work the center front three stitches in pattern (same as for the back) instead of purling them with both yarns held together for the steek, and work the neckband in the round on a 16" (40 cm) circular needle.

FINISHED SIZE
33 (35, 37, 39¾, 43, 46¼, 49¾)" (84 [89, 94, 101, 109, 117.5, 126.5] cm) bust circumference, buttoned. Sweater shown measures 35" (89 cm).

YARN
Sportweight (#2 Fine).

Shown here: Jamieson's Shetland Double Knitting (100% pure Shetland wool; 82 yd [75 m]/25 g): #235 grouse (dark brown heather; MC), 12 (13, 15, 16, 17, 19, 20) balls; #253 seaweed (gray-green heather; CC1), #429 old gold (greenish gold; CC2), and #1190 burnt umber (burnt orange heather; CC3), 2 (2, 2, 2, 3, 3, 3) balls each; #230 yellow ochre (yellow-gold heather; CC4), 1 (1, 1, 2, 2, 2, 2) ball(s).

NEEDLES
Ribbing, solid-color stockinette stitch, and edgings—size U.S. 4 (3.5 mm): 24" and 32" (60 and 80 cm) circular (cir) and set of 4 or 5 double-pointed (dpn). Areas of charted colorwork—size U.S. 5 (3.75 mm): 32" (80 cm) cir and set of 4 or 5 dpn. Adjust needle size if necessary to obtain the correct gauge.

NOTIONS
Markers (m); stitch holder; tapestry needle; sewing machine (optional); sharp-point sewing needle and matching thread; eleven (eleven, eleven, twelve, twelve, twelve, twelve) ⅜" (1 cm) buttons.

GAUGE
24 stitches and 32 rounds = 4" (10 cm) in stockinette stitch on smaller needles; 24 stitches and 24 rounds = 4" (10 cm) in charted colorwork pattern on larger needles, or in corrugated ribbing on smaller needles.

STITCH GUIDE

Long Corrugated Ribbing worked in Rounds (mult of 2 sts)
Rnd 1: *K1 with MC, k1 with CC1; rep from * to end.
Rnd 2: *K1 with MC, p1 with CC1; rep from * to end.
Rnds 3 and 4: *K1 with MC, p1 with CC2; rep from * to end.
Rnds 5 and 6: *K1 with MC, p1 with CC3; rep from * to end.
Rnds 7 and 8: *K1 with MC, p1 with CC4; rep from * to end.
Rnds 9 and 10: Rep Rnds 5 and 6.
Rnds 11 and 12: Rep Rnds 3 and 4.
Rnds 13 and 14: Rep Rnd 2.

Short Corrugated Ribbing worked in Rows (mult of 2 sts + 1)
Worked back and forth in rows—be sure to strand yarns on the WS of work (the side facing you) when working WS rows.
Row 1: (RS) K2 with MC, *k1 with CC1, k1 with MC; rep from * to last st, k1 with MC.
Row 2: (WS) P2 with MC, *k1 with CC2, p1 with MC; rep from * to last st, p1 with MC.
Row 3: K2 with MC, *p1 with CC3, k1 with MC; rep from * to last st, k1 with MC.
Row 4: P2 with MC, *k1 with CC4, p1 with MC; rep from * to last st, p1 with MC. Break MC and rejoin it to other side, ready to work another WS row (CC yarns will stay where they are).
Row 5: (WS) P2 with MC, *k1 with CC3, p1 with MC; rep from * to last st, p1 with MC.
Row 6: (RS) K2 with MC, *p1 with CC2, k1 with MC; rep from * to last st, k1 with MC.
Row 7: P2 with MC, *k1 with CC1, p1 with MC; rep from * to last st, p1 with MC.
Row 8: Cont with MC only, k2, *p1, k1; rep from * to last st, k1.

BODY

With MC and smaller long cir needle, CO 198 (210, 222, 238, 258, 278, 298) sts and *at the same time* place marker (pm) after the first 99 (105, 111, 119, 129, 139, 149) sts (for right underarm). Pm (for end of rnd and left underarm) and join for working in rnds, being careful not to twist sts. Work Rnds 1–14 of long corrugated ribbing (see Stitch Guide)—piece measures about 2½" (6.5 cm) from CO. Pm each side of front center 3 sts (omit for pullover option).
Dec rnd: Cont with MC, ssk, knit to center front 3 sts, p3 (knit these sts for pullover option), knit to 2 sts before next m, k2tog, slip m, ssk, knit to last 2 sts, k2tog—4 sts dec'd. Purling the center 3 sts every rnd, cont in St st and rep dec rnd every 3rd (3rd, 3rd, 3rd, 4th, 4th, 4th) rnd 2 (2, 2, 3, 2, 2, 2) more times, then every 3rd rnd 0 (0, 0, 0, 1, 1, 1) time—186 (198, 210, 222, 242, 262, 282) sts rem. Work 1 (1, 1, 0, 0, 0, 0) rnd even. *Next rnd:* Change to larger cir needle and, beg and end as indicated for your size, *work Rnd 1 of Body chart to patt rep box, rep patt rep box (noting that marked center front 3 sts are purled with both yarns held tog

on front only for cardigan steek) 5 (5, 7, 7, 7, 9, 9) times to 12 (15, 4, 7, 12, 3, 8) sts before right underarm marker, work sts outside patt rep to marker; rep from * across back sts (knitting center 3 sts rather than purling them). Work Rnds 2–12 of Body chart as established and *at the same time* rep dec rnd on Rnds 2, 5, 8, 10, and 12 for sizes 33", 35", and 37" only, and rep dec rnd on Rnds 3, 6, 9, and 12 for sizes 39¾", 43", 46¼", 49¾" only—83 (89, 95, 103, 113, 123, 133) sts rem each for front and back (including steek sts). Work Rnds 13–17 of chart even. *Inc rnd:* (Rnd 18 of chart) K1, M1R (see Glossary, page 137), work to 1 st before right underarm m, M1L (see Glossary, page 137), k2, M1R, work to last st, M1L, k1—4 sts inc'd. Cont in patt through Rnd 67 of chart and *at the same time* rep inc rnd every 6th rnd 7 more times, working new sts into patt, and ending 4 (5, 6, 7, 8, 9, 10) sts before end-of-rnd m—99 (105, 111, 119, 129, 139, 149) sts each for front and back (including steek sts); piece measures about 14¾ (14¾, 14¾, 15, 15¼, 15¼, 15¼)" (37.5 [37.5, 37.5, 38, 38.5, 38.5, 38.5] cm) from CO.

The background stays the same but the pattern colors shade from dark to light to dark.

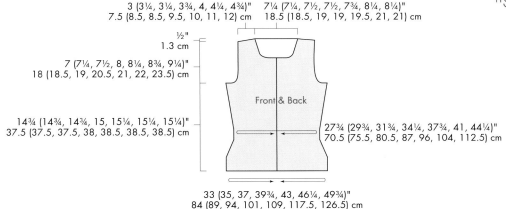

3 (3¼, 3¼, 3¾, 4, 4¼, 4¾)"
7.5 (8.5, 8.5, 9.5, 10, 11, 12) cm

7¼ (7¼, 7½, 7½, 7¾, 8¼, 8¼)"
18.5 (18.5, 19, 19, 19.5, 21, 21) cm

½"
1.3 cm

7 (7¼, 7½, 8, 8¼, 8¾, 9¼)"
18 (18.5, 19, 20.5, 21, 22, 23.5) cm

Front & Back

14¾ (14¾, 14¾, 15, 15¼, 15¼, 15¼)"
37.5 (37.5, 37.5, 38, 38.5, 38.5, 38.5) cm

27¾ (29¾, 31¾, 34¼, 37¾, 41, 44¼)"
70.5 (75.5, 80.5, 87, 96, 104, 112.5) cm

33 (35, 37, 39¾, 43, 46¼, 49¾)"
84 (89, 94, 101, 109, 117.5, 126.5) cm

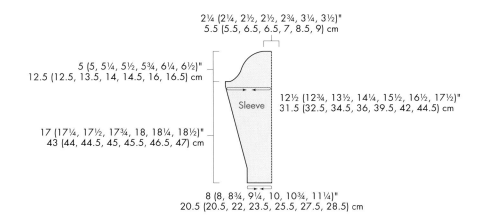

2¼ (2¼, 2½, 2½, 2¾, 3¼, 3½)"
5.5 (5.5, 6.5, 6.5, 7, 8.5, 9) cm

5 (5, 5¼, 5½, 5¾, 6¼, 6½)"
12.5 (12.5, 13.5, 14, 14.5, 16, 16.5) cm

12½ (12¾, 13½, 14¼, 15½, 16½, 17½)"
31.5 (32.5, 34.5, 36, 39.5, 42, 44.5) cm

Sleeve

17 (17¼, 17½, 17¾, 18, 18¼, 18½)"
43 (44, 44.5, 45, 45.5, 46.5, 47) cm

8 (8, 8¾, 9¼, 10, 10¾, 11¼)"
20.5 (20.5, 22, 23.5, 25.5, 27.5, 28.5) cm

Divide for Front and Back

P1, BO 1 steek st (2 sts on right needle), sl m, k31 (32, 33, 35, 37, 39, 41), join new ball of yarn and BO center 15 (15, 17, 17, 19, 21, 21) sts (including center front steek sts), work to right arm-hole m, p2. Place rem 77 (79, 83, 87, 93, 99, 103) back sts plus 1 purl st at each end of back (one of these will be the former first st of the rnd) on holder to work later—79 (81, 85, 89, 95, 101, 105) back sts total.

FRONT

Work front sts back in forth in rows, working each side separately as foll: With WS facing, BO 1 steek st at beg of row—32 (33, 34, 36, 38, 40, 42) sts rem each side. There is 1 steek st at each end of needle; these are now selvedge sts. At each neck edge, BO 4 sts once, then BO 3 sts once, then BO 2 sts 2 times, then dec 1 st every RS row 3 times—18 (19, 20, 22, 24, 26, 28) sts rem each side. Cont even until armholes measure 7 (7¼, 7½, 8, 8¼, 8¾, 9¼)" (18 [18.5, 19, 20.5, 21, 22, 23.5] cm), ending with a WS row.

Shape Shoulders

At each armhole edge, BO 9 (10, 10, 11, 12, 13, 14) sts once, then BO rem 9 (9, 10, 11, 12, 13, 14) sts.

BACK

Place 79 (81, 85, 89, 95, 101, 105) held back sts onto smaller needle and join MC, ready to work a RS row. Working back and forth in rows, work even in St st until piece measures same as front to shoulders, ending with a WS row.

Shape Neck and Shoulders

Mark center 39 (39, 41, 41, 43, 45, 45) sts. *Next row:* (RS) BO 9 (10, 10, 11, 12, 13, 14) sts, work to marked center sts, join new ball of yarn and BO center 39 (39, 41, 41, 43, 45, 45) sts, work to end—11 (11, 12, 13, 14, 15, 16) sts rem for right side and 20 (21, 22, 24, 26, 28, 30) sts rem for left side. *Note:* The neck is shaped at the same time as the shoulders; read all the way through the foll section before proceeding. Working each side separately, at left armhole edge BO 9 (10, 10, 11, 12, 13, 14) sts once, then BO 9 (9, 10, 11, 12, 13, 14) sts at each armhole edge once and *at the same time* at each neck edge BO 2 sts once—no sts rem when all shaping is complete.

SLEEVES

With smaller dpn, CO 48 (48, 52, 56, 60, 64, 68) sts. Divide sts evenly among 3 or 4 needles, pm, and join for working in rnds, being careful not to twist sts. Work Rnds 1–14 of long corrugated ribbing worked in rnds—piece measures about 2½" (6.5 cm) from CO. *Next rnd:* (RS) With MC, k24 (24, 26, 28, 30, 32, 34), M1L, knit to end—49 (49, 53, 57, 61, 65, 69) sts. Work 7 (7, 7, 7, 6, 6, 6) rnds even in St st. *Inc rnd:* K1, M1R, knit to last st, M1L, k1—2 sts inc'd. Rep inc rnd every 8 (8, 8, 8, 7, 7, 7)th rnd 8 (8, 8, 7, 10, 7, 3) more times, then every 7th rnd 0 (0, 0, 2, 0, 0, 0) times, then every 6th rnd 0 (0, 0, 0, 0, 4, 9) times—67 (67, 71, 77, 83, 89, 95) sts. Work 2 (4, 6, 2, 5, 4, 4) rnds even—piece measures about 11¾ (12, 12¼, 12½, 12¾, 13, 13¼)" (30 [30.5, 31, 31.5, 32.5, 33, 33.5] cm) from CO. Change to larger dpn and, beg and end as indicated for your size (see Notes), work Rnds 1–26 of Sleeve chart and *at the same time* rep inc rnd on Rnds 5, 12, 19, and 26 for sizes 33" and 39¾" only, and rep inc rnd on Rnds 2, 8, 14, 20, and 26 for sizes 35", 37", 43", 46¼", and 49¾" only—75 (77, 81, 85, 93, 99, 105) sts after Rnd 26. Change to MC and smaller dpn. Work 7 rnds even, ending 4 (5, 6, 7, 8, 9, 10) sts before end-of-rnd m—piece measures about 17 (17¼, 17½, 17¾, 18, 18¼, 18½)" (43 [44, 44.5, 45, 45.5, 46.5, 47] cm) from CO.

Shape Cap

BO next 8 (10, 12, 14, 16, 18, 20) sts, knit to end—67 (67, 69, 71, 77, 81, 85) sts rem. Working back and forth in rows, purl 1 (WS) row. *Dec row:* (RS) K1, ssk, knit to last 3 sts, k2tog, k1—2 sts dec'd. Rep dec row every other row 8 (8, 7, 6, 9, 9, 9) more times, then every 4th row 1 (1, 2, 2, 1, 2, 2) time(s), then every other row 4 (4, 4, 6, 6, 6, 7) times—39 (39, 41, 41, 43, 45, 47) sts rem. BO 2 sts at beg of next 4 rows, then BO 3 sts at beg of foll 6 rows—13 (13, 15, 15, 17, 19, 21) sts rem. BO all sts.

Corrugated ribbing (alternating colors every stitch) is a nice way to add color to edgings.

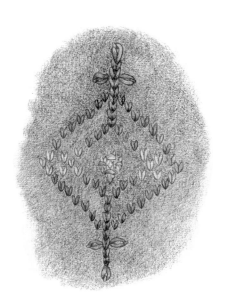

Use embroidery to
add bits of color to
isolated areas.

CARDIGAN FINISHING

Weave in loose ends. Block pieces to measurements.

Cut Steeks

Turn garment inside out (steeks will appear as 3 knit sts on WS). Machine-stitch (or hand-stitch with sewing needle and thread) two lines of closely spaced sts on each side of center of armhole and center front steeks (purled steek sts end at ribbing on center front; cont to lower edge of ribbing in line with steek sts). Carefully cut between lines of sts on each steek.

Embroidery

With CC3 threaded on a tapestry needle, work 3 individual chain sts (see Glossary, page 135) at top and bottom of pointed Fair Isle motifs on front, back, and sleeves as shown at left.

Attach Sleeves

With MC threaded on a tapestry needle, sew fronts to back at shoulders. Turn garment inside out. Place right-side-out sleeve inside garment so that RS face tog, matching underarms and top of cap to shoulder seam. Pin in place, distributing ease over shoulder area. With MC threaded on a tapestry needle, sew in place. Rep for other sleeve.

Collar

With MC, smaller cir needle, RS facing, and beg at right front neck edge, pick up and knit 1 st in cut steek, 31 (31, 32, 32, 33, 34, 34) sts along right front neck edge, 45 (45, 47, 47, 49, 51, 51) sts across back neck edge, 31 (31, 32, 32, 33, 34, 34) sts along left front neck edge, and 1 st in cut steek—109 (109, 113, 113, 117, 121, 121) sts total. Do not join. Purl 1 WS row, dec 22 (22, 22, 22, 24, 24, 24) sts evenly spaced—87 (87, 91, 91, 93, 97, 97) sts rem. Work Rows 1–8 of short corrugated ribbing worked in rows (see Stitch Guide). BO all sts in patt.

Buttonband

With MC, smaller cir needle, RS facing, and beg at top of left front collar, pick up and knit 10 sts along collar (working between the 2 MC knit sts), 12 (14, 16, 18, 19, 23, 25) sts along plain MC section (working into 3 out of every 4 rows and picking up between steek and first knit st), 82 sts along Fair Isle section (working into every row), 6 (6, 6, 8, 9, 9, 9) sts along plain section to top of ribbing (working into 3 out of every 4 rows), and 15 sts along long corrugated ribbing edge (working into every row)—125 (127, 129, 133, 135, 139, 141) sts total.

Row 1: (WS) Stranding yarns on WS, p2 with MC, *k1 with CC1, p1 with MC; rep from * to last st, sl 1 with yarn in front (wyf).

Row 2: (RS) K2 with MC, *p1 with CC2, k1 with MC; rep from * to last st, sl 1 with yarn in back (wyb).

Row 3: With MC, p2, *k1, p1; rep from * to last st, sl 1 wyf.

BO all sts in patt.

Buttonhole Band

With MC, smaller cir needle, RS facing, and beg at lower right front, pick up and knit sts as for buttonband, but working in reverse order—125 (127, 129, 133, 135, 139, 141) sts.

Row 1: (WS) P2 with MC, *k1 with CC1, p1 with MC; rep from * to last st, sl 1 wyf.

Row 2: (RS; buttonhole row) K2 with MC, [p1 with CC2, k1 with MC] 0 (1, 1, 0, 1, 1, 1) time, [yo with CC2, k2tog with MC, (p1 with CC2, k1 with MC) 5 times] 10 (10, 10, 10, 10, 11, 11) times, [yo with CC2, k2tog with MC, (p1 with CC2, k1 with MC) 3 times] 0 (0, 0, 1, 1, 0, 0) time, yo with CC2, k2tog with MC, [p1 with CC2, k1 with MC] 0 (0, 1, 0, 0, 0, 1) time, sl 1 wyb.

Row 3: With MC, p2, *k1, p1; rep from * to last st, sl 1 wyf.
BO all sts in patt.

Sew buttons to left front, opposite buttonholes. Press center front steek edges to inside, using a damp press cloth and steam iron on wool setting. Work trefoils of chain sts around cuff and collar edges where ribbing meets main fabric (as shown in photo), centered on outside point of sleeves and back neck, and working them 2" (5 cm) apart (center to center) all around. With sharp-point sewing needle and thread, hand-sew steek edges neatly to inside edges of cardigan (see page 126).

PULLOVER FINISHING

Work as for cardigan finishing, omitting sewing and cutting of front center steek, and button-bands.

Collar

With MC, smaller dpn, RS facing, and beg at right shoulder edge, pick up and knit 45 (45, 47, 47, 49, 51, 51) sts across back neck edge and 65 (65, 67, 67, 69, 71, 71) sts across front neck edge—110 (110, 114, 114, 118, 122, 122) sts total. Pm and join for working in rnds. Knit 1 rnd, dec 22 (22, 22, 22, 24, 24, 24) sts evenly spaced—88 (88, 92, 92, 94, 98, 98) sts rem. Work Rnds 1, 3, 5, 7, 9, 11, and 13 (i.e., omit even-numbered rnds) of long corrugated ribbing worked in rnds (see Stitch Guide). With MC, *k1, p1; rep from * to end. BO all sts in patt.

Plan your garment with Fair Isle patterns worked in rounds so you don't have to worry about following the chart on wrong-side rows.

Kristin Nicholas is an expert at colorwork. In this clever hooded scarf, she knitted a very wide short tube (in rounds). She began with several rounds of garter stitch to make a non-curling edge, then worked colorful stripes in reverse stockinette stitch (knitting the color-change-rounds for clean demarcation of the stripes), followed by a simple Fair Isle pattern. At the center, she reversed the stripe pattern, then ended with several rounds of garter stitch. To finish, she cut the tube and raveled several rows to create a fringe; then she embroidered whimsical flowers and vines along the Fair Isle portion, sewed the center together to form a hood, and added a colorful tassel.

STITCH GUIDE

Reverse Stockinette Ridge
Rnd 1: Knit.
Rnds 2 and 3: K10, purl to last 10 sts, k10.
Repeat Rounds 1–3 for pattern.

NOTE
✦ The scarf is worked in the round so that the cast-on and bind-off edges form the long sides. After the knitting is complete, the tube is cut open and the cut edges become the short ends of the scarf. Stitches are raveled along the short ends to create the fringe, then the hood section is sewn together.

FINISHED SIZE
About 9" (23 cm) wide and 41" (104 cm) long from top of hood to end of scarf, not including fringe.

YARN
Worsted weight (#4 Medium).

Shown here: Nashua Handknits Julia (50% wool, 25% mohair, 25% alpaca; 93 yd [85 m]/50 g): #NHJ3961 lady's mantle (chartreuse), 3 balls; #NHJ8141 pretty pink (pink) and #NHJ2230 rock henna (brick red), 2 balls each; #NHJ2083 magenta, #NHJ6086 velvet moss (dark olive), #NHJ2250 French pumpkin (orange), and #NHJ6396 deep blue sea (teal), 1 ball each.

NEEDLES
Sizes U.S. 8 and 7 (5 and 4.5 mm): 32" (80 cm) circular (cir). Adjust needle size if necessary to obtain the correct gauge.

NOTIONS
Markers (m); tapestry needle; scissors.

GAUGE
18 stitches and 27 rows = 4" (10 cm) in pattern from Diamond chart on larger needle; 18 stitches and 36 rows = 4" (10 cm) in reverse stockinette ridge pattern on smaller needle.

SCARF

With pink and smaller cir needle, CO 388 sts, maintaining even tension. Place marker (pm) and join for working in rnds, being careful not to twist sts. *Next rnd:* K10, pm, p368, pm, k10. The first and last 10 sts are knitted every rnd and will be raveled later for fringe. Knit 1 rnd. Rep the last 2 rnds once more, then work the first rnd again. Work Rnds 1–3 of reverse stockinette ridge (see Stitch Guide) with brick red, then chartreuse, then magenta, then dark olive, then orange, then teal—piece measures about 2¾" (7 cm) from CO. Change to larger cir needle and work Rows 1–8 of Diamond chart 3 times—piece measures about 3½" (9 cm) from beg of charted patt. Change to smaller cir needle and work Rnds 1–3 of reverse stockinette ridge with teal, then orange, then dark olive, then magenta, then chartreuse, then brick red. Change to pink and knit 1 rnd. *Next rnd:* K10, p368, k10. *Next rnd:* Knit. Rep the last 2 rnds once more, then rep the purl rnd again—3 garter ridges; piece measures 9" (23 cm) from CO. BO all sts, matching tension of CO edge.

Work woven web circles framed with daisy stitches and connected with undulating stem stitches along the Fair Isle center of the scarf.

FINISHING

Fringe

With sharp scissors, cut the scarf open at beg of rnd, exactly in the center of the 20 stockinette fringe sts; do not cut near the charted pattern areas. Using a knitting needle or tapestry needle and beg at the BO edge, carefully ravel 6 rnds of sts from the 10-st fringe section at each end of scarf. Tie each bundle of raveled ends into an overhand knot, snug against the end of the charted patt. Rep for each 6 rnds to CO edge of scarf.

Embroidery

Foll the illustration below left, work 1" (2.5 cm) woven web circles (see Glossary, pages 135–136, for embroidery instructions) every 5" (12.5 cm) in pink, magenta, and orange, beginning and ending about 2" (5 cm) from the fringed edge. With the same colors, work 9 or 10 individual chain sts around each circle, and with the same yarn doubled, work a French knot in the center of each spider web circle. With 2 strands of teal, work undulating stem stitches between the circles, then work straight sts to form leaves.

Weave in loose ends. Spritz scarf with water, especially the kinked strands of fringe, and steam-block to even out the charted colorwork section and straighten the fringe. Alternatively, handwash the scarf according to the label instructions and dry flat, smoothing the colorwork section and fringe by hand.

Hood

Fold scarf in half widthwise. With pink threaded on a tapestry needle and beg at fold, use a whipstitch (see Glossary, page 139) to sew CO edge tog for about 8" (20.5 cm) to form back of hood.

Tassel

With chartreuse, magenta, and teal, make a thick 3¾" (9.5 cm) tassel (see Glossary, page 139). Cut 6 strands of assorted colors (omitting dark olive and teal), each about 10" (25.5 cm) long. Holding 2 yarns tog for each group, use the 6 strands to make a 3-strand braid to make a tie to attach the tassel to the tip of the "hood."

Work stripes in reverse stockinette stitch and the color-change rows in stockinette stitch to give a corduroy effect.

Diamond

	brick red
+	chartreuse
	pattern repeat

Pam Allen started her bag on small double-pointed needles to form a sturdy garter-stitch base. When the circular base was big enough around, she switched to a larger circular needle and a repeating Fair Isle pattern. To create more color play, she intermittently changed the background and pattern colors but kept the light-dark contrast fairly constant. The bag ends at the top edge with a striped garter rib. The shoulder strap continues on stitches left open at the top edge of the bag; it's shaped at the bag ends with full-fashioned decreases.

BAG

Bottom

With A and dpn, CO 9 sts. Divide sts evenly onto 3 needles. Place marker (pm) and join for working in rnds, being careful not to twist sts. Knit 1 rnd. *Inc Rnd 1:* *Knit into front and back of next st (k1f&b); rep from * to end—18 sts. Purl 1 rnd, then knit 1 rnd, then purl 1 rnd. *Inc Rnd 2:* *K1f&b; rep from * to end—36 sts. [Purl 1 rnd, then knit 1 rnd] 3 times, purl 1 rnd. Rep Inc Rnd 2—72 sts. [Purl 1 rnd, then knit 1 rnd] 6 times, purl 1 rnd, changing to 16" (40 cm) cir needle when there are too many sts to fit comfortably on dpn. Rep Inc Rnd 2—144 sts. [Purl 1 rnd, then knit 1 rnd] 3 times, purl 1 rnd. *Next rnd:* *K6, M1 (see Glossary, page 137); rep from * to end of rnd—168 sts.

Sides

Change to larger cir needle. Cont in St st (knit every rnd), work Rnds 1–14 of Fair Isle chart 4 times, then work Rnd 1 once more (57 rnds total), as foll:
Rnds 1–9: A for MC; C for CC.
Rnds 10–14 and Rnds 1–7: A for MC; D for CC.
Rnds 8–13: A for MC; E for CC.
Rnd 14 and Rnds 1–9: A for MC; C for CC.
Rnds 10–14 and Rnd 1: A for MC; D for CC.
Rnd 2: B for MC; D for CC.
Rnds 3–10: B for MC; E for CC.
Rnd 11: B for MC; F for CC.
Rnds 12–14 and Rnd 1: A for MC; F for CC.

FINISHED SIZE
About 16" (40.5 cm) wide and 17" (43 cm) tall, excluding strap.

YARN
Worsted weight (#4 Medium).

Shown here: Classic Elite Renaissance (100% wool; 110 yd [101 m]/50 g): #7178 tiled roof (rust; A), #7155 Renaissance red (dark red; B), #7181 green grape (olive; C), #7135 celery (pale green; D), #7168 Vatican gold (E), #7172 green pepper (bright green; F), #7185 portofino orange (G), and #7124 giotto grape (purple; H), 1 skein each.

NEEDLES
Bag base—size U.S. 6 (4 mm): set of 4 double-pointed (dpn) and 16" (40 cm) circular (cir). Bag sides—size U.S. 7 (4.5 mm): 24" (60 cm) cir. Adjust needle size if necessary to obtain the correct gauge.

NOTIONS
Markers (m); large holder or waste yarn; tapestry needle.

GAUGE
21 stitches and 22 rows = 4" (10 cm) in Fair Isle pattern on larger needle.

Change colors at different places in the pattern repeat for more visual interest.

With A, knit 1 rnd. Remove marker, k42, pm for new beg of rnd. *Next rnd:* P1,*k2, p2; rep from * to last 3 sts, k2, p1. *Next rnd:* Knit. Rep the last 2 rnds 2 more times. Change to G and work 4 rnds as established, ending 4 sts before m on last rnd.

Shape Top and Strap

Place a marker at the halfway point (between the 84th and 85th sts)—there will be 1 purl st on each side of marker. *Next rnd:* BO 8 sts, work in patt to 4 sts before next m, BO 8 sts, work in patt to end of rnd—76 sts rem for each side. Place first 76 sts on holder or waste yarn to work later. *Next row:* Turn work so WS is facing and work in patt as established to end of row. *Note:* Strap shaping is introduced at the same time the stripe patt is worked; read all the way through the foll section before proceeding. *Dec row:* (RS) K3, p2, k1, ssk, work to last 8 sts, k2tog, k1, p2, k3—2 sts dec'd. *Next row:* Work the sts as they appear (knit the knits and purl the purls). Rep the last 2 rows working the stripe patt as foll:

2 rows with G (8 rows total).
4 rows with C.
2 rows with H.
5 rows with A.
2 rows with E.
4 rows with A.
3 rows with D.
4 rows with G.
6 rows with B.
2 rows with F.
5 rows with E.
2 rows with H.
5 rows with A.
3 rows with E for first strap; 3 rows with C for second strap.
4 rows with G.
2 rows with C.
4 rows with B.
2 rows with G.
3 rows with B.
4 rows with D.
3 rows with H.
2 rows with E.
2 rows with H.
5 rows with G.

At the same time, when 16 sts rem, ending with a WS row, work strap as foll: (RS) K3, p2, k6, p2, k3. *Next row*: P3, k2, p6, k2, p3. Rep the last 2 rows through the end of the stripe sequence, then change to B and work even until piece measures 13½" (34.5 cm) from first BO rnd. Place sts on holder. Return 76 held sts onto needle. With WS facing, join G and work 1 row even. Beg with dec row, work second strap as for first.

FINISHING

Using the three-needle method (see Glossary, page 133), BO the ends of strap tog. Weave in loose ends. Steam-block lightly.

Fair Isle

- ☐ MC (see instructions)
- ☒ CC (see instructions)
- ☐ pattern repeat

MOSAIC YOKE JACKET
VÉRONIK AVERY

Véronik Avery has followed the silhouette of retro-style tailored jackets with notched collars and circular yoke shaping for this trim jacket. The body is worked in one piece from the hem to the shoulders, with the sleeves added along the way. Vertical stripes formed by slipped stitches follow the lower body and sleeves to the yoke where Véronik switched to stripes in the background to give the look of a Fair Isle pattern. The double-thick edging around the fronts and lower body is worked in one piece, with increases used to round the corners and short-rows used to shape the lapels and collar. For an unexpected splash of color, the hems of the three-quarter-length sleeves are punctuated with a single row of blue-violet stitches.

STITCH GUIDE

Vertical Tweed Pattern in Rows (mult of 4 sts + 1)

Row 1: (RS) With CC, *sl 1 purlwise with yarn in back (pwise wyb), p1, k1, p1; rep from * to last st, sl 1 pwise wyb.

Row 2: With CC, *sl 1 pwise with yarn in front (wyf), p1, k1, p1; rep from * to last st, sl 1 pwise wyf.

Row 3: With MC, *k1, p1; rep from * to last st, k1.

Row 4: With MC, *p2, k1, p1; rep from * to last st, p1.

Repeat Rows 1–4 for pattern.

Vertical Tweed Pattern in Rounds (mult of 4 sts)

Rnd 1: With CC, *sl 1 pwise wyb, p1, k1, p1; rep from * to end.

Rnd 2: With CC, *sl 1 pwise wyb, k1, p1, k1; rep from * to end.

Rnd 3: With MC, *k1, p1; rep from * to end.

Rnd 4: With MC, *k2, p1, k1; rep from * to end.

Repeat Rounds 1–4 for pattern.

FINISHED SIZE
About 32 (35½, 39, 42¾, 46¼)" (81.5 [90, 99, 108.5, 117.5] cm) bust circumference. Sweater shown measures 35½" (90 cm).

YARN
Worsted weight (#4 Medium).

Shown here: Reynolds Lite Lopi (100% wool; 109 yd [100 m]/50 g): #59 (black; MC), 5 (6, 7, 8, 9) balls; #57 (gray; CC), 4 (4, 5, 6, 6) balls; #427 rust heather (A), #53 acorn (medium brown; B), #264 mustard (C), #304 blue violet (D), and #54 ash (off white; E), 1 ball each.

NEEDLES
Sizes U.S. 5 and 7 (3.75 and 4.5 mm): 32" (80 cm) circular (cir) and set of 4 or 5 double-pointed (dpn). Adjust needle size if necessary to obtain the correct gauge.

NOTIONS
Markers (m); stitch holders; waste yarn for provisional cast-on; tapestry needle.

GAUGE
18 stitches and 34 rows = 4" (10 cm) in vertical tweed pattern on smaller needle; 21 stitches and 52 rows = 4" (10 cm) in charted mosaic pattern on larger needle.

Work a slip-stitch pattern in stripes to give the look of Fair Isle patterning.

NOTES

✤ The body is worked in one piece to the armholes, then the sleeves are added and the yoke is worked in one piece to the neck.

✤ The collar and lapels are shaped with short-rows using yarnovers at the turning points. To hide gaps on right-side rows: Knit to 1 stitch before gap, k2tog (1 stitch each side of gap). To hide gaps on wrong-side rows: Purl to 1 stitch before gap, ssp (1 stitch each side of gap; see Glossary, page 134).

✤ The yoke design is worked in the slip-stitch technique (see Design Notebook) of using only one color per two rows (the color indicated in the bar to the right of the chart). Knit the stitches in the indicated color on the chart and slip the stitches in the other color (with the yarn in back on right-side rows; in front on wrong-side rows). Each two-row sequence is represented by one row on the chart.

BODY

With MC, smaller cir needle, and using a provisional method (see Glossary, page 133), CO 135 (151, 167, 183, 199) sts. Do not join. Purl 1 (WS) row. Break yarn, leaving a 12" (30.5 cm) tail. Work as foll:

Row 1: Sl 9 sts to right needle without knitting them, join CC and work Row 1 of vertical tweed patt in rows (see Stitch Guide) to last 9 sts, turn work (leave last 9 sts unworked).

Row 2: Yo, work in patt as established to last 6 sts, turn work.

Row 3: Keeping in patt, rejoin MC, yo, work to 1 st before gap from previous row, k2tog (yo and next st), work to last 6 sts, turn work.

Row 4: Keeping in patt, yo, work to 1 st before gap from previous row, ssp, work to last 2 sts, turn work.

Row 5: With CC and cont in patt, yo, work to 1 st before gap from previous row, k2tog, work to last 2 sts, turn work.

Rows 6 and 7: Cont in patt, work to last st, closing gaps as before, then work last st in St st.

Next row: (WS) P1 (selvedge st; work in St st throughout), work 133 (149, 165, 181, 197) sts in patt as established, p1 (selvedge st; work in St st throughout). Cont in patt as established until piece measures 1¼ (1¼, 1¼, 1¾, 1¾)" (3.2 [3.2, 3.2, 4.5, 4.5] cm) from CO, ending with Row 1 of patt. *Next row:* Work 30 (34, 38, 42, 46) sts in patt, place marker (pm), work 3 sts, pm, work 69 (77, 85, 93, 101) sts, pm, work 3 sts, pm, work to end.

Shape Waist

(Row 3 of patt) Keeping in patt, *work to 2 sts before m, k2tog, slip marker (sl m), work 3 sts, sl m, ssk; rep from * once more, work to end of row—4 sts dec'd. Work 3 rows even. Rep the last 4 rows once more—127 (143, 159, 175, 191) sts rem. *Next row:* Keeping in patt, *work to 3 sts before m, k3tog, sl m, work 3 sts, sl m, sssk (see Glossary, page 134); rep from * once more, work to end of row—119 (135, 151, 167, 183) sts rem. Work even until piece measures 3½ (3½, 3½, 4, 4)" (9 [9, 9, 10, 10] cm) from CO, ending with Row 2 of patt.

Shape Upper Body

(Row 3 of patt) Keeping in patt, *work to 1 st before m, (k1, yo, k1) in next st, sl m, work 3 sts, sl m, (k1, yo, k1) in next st; rep from * once more, work to end of row—127 (143, 159, 175, 191) sts. Work 7 rows even. *Next row:* *Work to 1 st before m, M1 (see Glossary, page 137), k1, sl m, work 3 sts, sl m, k1, M1; rep from * once more, work to end of row—4 sts inc'd. Work 7 rows even, then rep last inc row once more—135 (151, 167, 183, 199) sts. Work even until piece measures 11 (11½, 12, 12¼, 12¾)" (28 [29, 30.5, 31, 32.5] cm) from CO, ending with Row 3 of patt. *Next row:* (WS; Row 4 of patt) Keeping in patt, work 38 (42, 46, 50, 54) sts, then sl the last 12 of these sts onto a holder for left under-arm, work 72 (80, 88, 96, 104) sts, then sl the last 12 of these sts onto a second holder for right underarm, work to end—26 (30, 34, 38, 42) sts rem for left front; 60 (68, 76, 84, 92) sts rem for back; 25 (29, 33, 37, 41) sts rem for right front. Do not cut yarn. Set aside.

SLEEVES

With MC, smaller dpn, and using a provisional method, CO 48 (52, 56, 64, 68) sts. Divide sts evenly onto 3 or 4 dpn, pm, and join for working in rnds, being careful not to twist sts. Work 18 rnds even. Knit 1 rnd with D. Purl 1 rnd with MC for turning ridge, knit 18 rnds, then purl 1 rnd. Join CC and work vertical tweed patt in rnds (see Stitch Guide) until piece measures 4 (4, 4, 5, 5)" (10 [10, 10, 12.5, 12.5] cm) from turning ridge, ending with Rnd 2 of patt. *Inc Rnd 1:* (Rnd 3 of patt) (K1, yo, k1) in next st, work to end—50 (54, 58, 66, 70) sts. Work 11 rnds even. *Inc Rnd 2:* [K1, M1] 2 times, work to end—52 (56, 60, 68, 72) sts. Work 11 rnds even. *Inc Rnd 3:* (K1, yo, k1) in next st, work 3 sts in patt, (k1, yo, k1) in next st, work to end—56 (60, 64, 72, 76) sts. Work 11 rnds even. *Inc Rnd 4:* K1, M1, work 6 sts in patt, M1, work to end—58 (62, 66, 74, 78) sts. Work 11 rnds even. *Inc Rnd 5:* K1, M1, work 7 sts in patt, M1, work to end—60 (64, 68, 76, 80) sts. Work even until piece measures 10 (10, 10, 11, 11)" (25.5 [25.5, 25.5, 28, 28] cm) from turning ridge, ending with Rnd 3 of patt. *Next rnd:* (Rnd 4 of patt) Work 12 sts, then sl these sts onto a holder, work to end—48 (52, 56, 64, 68) sts rem.

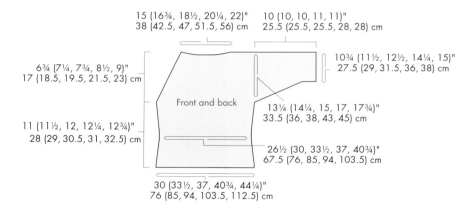

15 (16¾, 18½, 20¼, 22)"
38 (42.5, 47, 51.5, 56) cm

10 (10, 10, 11, 11)"
25.5 (25.5, 25.5, 28, 28) cm

6¾ (7¼, 7¾, 8½, 9)"
17 (18.5, 19.5, 21.5, 23) cm

10¾ (11½, 12½, 14¼, 15)"
27.5 (29, 31.5, 36, 38) cm

Front and back

13¼ (14¼, 15, 17, 17¾)"
33.5 (36, 38, 43, 45) cm

11 (11½, 12, 12¼, 12¾)"
28 (29, 30.5, 31, 32.5) cm

26½ (30, 33½, 37, 40¾)"
67.5 (76, 85, 94, 103.5) cm

30 (33½, 37, 40¾, 44¼)"
76 (85, 94, 103.5, 112.5) cm

YOKE

With smaller cir needle and using yarn attached to body, cont in patt across 25 (29, 33, 37, 41) right front sts, 48 (52, 56, 64, 68) right sleeve sts, 60 (68, 76, 84, 92) back sts, 48 (52, 56, 64, 68) left sleeve sts, and 26 (30, 34, 38, 42) left front sts—207 (231, 255, 287, 311) sts total. Work in patt until yoke measures ¼ (½, 1, 1¾, 2¼)" (6 mm [1.3, 2.5, 4.5, 5.5] cm), ending with Row 2 of patt. Cont in MC only, knit 2 rows, dec 2 (2, 2, 18, 18) sts evenly spaced on last row—205 (229, 253, 269, 293) sts rem. Change to larger cir needle. *Note:* The neckline shaping is introduced at the same time as the yoke patt is worked; read all the way through the foll section before proceeding. *Set-up row:* (RS) K1 (selvedge st; work in St st throughout), work 8-st patt rep of Yoke chart 25 (28, 31, 33, 36) times (see Notes), work next

Choose a round yoke shaping for uninterrupted color patterning.

3 sts as indicated on chart, k1 (selvedge st; work in St st throughout). Cont in patt, work Rows 2–49 of chart, working a double dec in each patt rep as indicated on Row 49. *At the same time* dec 1 st at each neck edge on Row 19 of chart, then every 4th row (every other row of chart) 7 more times—143 (161, 179, 191, 209) sts rem after Row 49. Change to smaller cir needle and with MC, knit 1 (WS) row, dec 0 (2, 4, 0, 2) sts evenly spaced—143 (159, 175, 191, 207) sts rem. Cont shaping neck as foll:

Row 1: K1 (selvedge st), work vertical tweed patt across next 141 (157, 173, 189, 205) sts, k1 (selvedge st).

Row 2 and all WS rows: Work even in patt.

Row 3: K1, ssk, work to last 3 sts, k2tog, k1—141 (157, 173, 189, 205) sts rem.

Rows 5, 9, 13, and 17: Work even in patt.

Row 7: K1, ssk, p1, *k1, p3tog, [k1, p1] 2 times; rep from * to last 9 sts, k1, p3tog, k1, p1, k2tog, k1—105 (117, 129, 141, 153) sts rem.

Rows 11 and 15: Rep Row 3—101 (113, 125, 137, 149) sts rem after Row 15.

Row 19: K1, *k3tog, p1, k1, p1; rep from * to last 4 sts, k3tog, k1—67 (75, 83, 91, 99) sts rem. Cont even in patt until yoke measures 6¾ (7¼, 7¾, 8½, 9)" (17 [18.5, 19.5, 21.5, 23] cm). Place sts on holder.

Yoke

◆	MC
◎	A
◇	B
I	C
□	D
·	E
⋏	with MC, sl 1, k2tog, psso
	no stitch
	pattern repeat

Only one color is used for each row of a slip-stitch pattern.

FINISHING

With MC threaded on a tapestry needle, use Kitchener st (see Glossary, page 136) to graft underarm sts tog. Weave in loose ends.

Lapels, Facings, and Hem

Remove waste yarn from provisional CO at lower body edge and carefully place live sts onto a needle. With MC, smaller cir needle, RS facing, and beg on left front at top of yoke patt, pick up and knit 68 (72, 76, 80, 86) sts along left front, pm, k134 (150, 166, 182, 198) exposed sts from CO edge, pm, and pick up and knit 68 (72, 76, 80, 86) sts along right front to top of yoke patt—270 (294, 318, 342, 370) sts total. Do not join. Knit 1 (WS) row. Work 2 rows even in St st. *Next row:* *Knit to 5 sts before m, [M1, k2] 2 times, M1, k1, sl m, k1, [M1, k2] 2 times, M1; rep from * once more, knit to end of row—12 sts inc'd. Work 1 WS row even. Rep the last 2 rows once more—294 (318, 342, 366, 394) sts.

Shape Bottom Left Lapel

Row 1: K3, k2tog, k25, turn—1 st dec'd.
Row 2: Yo, purl to end.
Row 3: K3, k2tog, knit to 6 sts before gap formed on previous row, turn—1 st dec'd.
Rep Rows 2 and 3 three more times, then work Row 2 once more—289 (313, 337, 361, 389) sts rem. Knit across all sts, closing gaps as you come to them (see Notes).

Shape Bottom Right Lapel

Row 1: (WS) P30, turn.
Row 2: Yo, knit to last 5 sts, ssk, k3—1 st dec'd.
Row 3: Purl to 6 sts before gap formed on previous row, turn.
Rep Rows 2 and 3 three more times, then rep Row 2 once more—284 (308, 332, 356, 384) sts rem. Purl across all sts, closing gaps as you come to them (see Notes). Knit 2 rows even for turning ridge.

Shape Top Left Lapel

Row 1: K5, turn.
Row 2: Yo, purl to end.
Row 3: K3, M1, knit to 1 st before gap formed on previous row, k2tog, k4, turn—1 st inc'd.
Rep Rows 2 and 3 three more times. *Next row:* K3, M1, knit to 1 st before gap, k2tog, knit to end of row—289 (313, 337, 361, 389) sts.

Shape Top Right Lapel

Row 1: (WS) P5, turn.

Row 2: Yo, knit to last 3 sts, M1, knit to end—1 st inc'd.

Row 3: Purl to 1 st before gap, ssp, p4, turn.

Rep Rows 2 and 3 three more times, then rep Row 2 once more—294 (318, 342, 366, 394) sts. Purl to 1 st before gap, ssp, purl to end of row. *Dec row:* *Knit to 5 sts before m, k2tog, k1, k2tog, sl m, k2tog, k1, k2tog; rep from * once more, knit to end of row—8 sts dec'd. Purl 1 row. Rep dec row once more—278 (302, 326, 350, 378) sts rem. Work 7 rows even. With RS facing, BO all sts.

Collar

With MC, smaller cir needle, and RS facing, pick up and knit 8 sts along selvedge of bottom right lapel, 10 sts along right front, k67 (75, 83, 91, 99) held neck sts, pick up and knit 10 sts along left front, and 8 sts along selvedge of bottom left lapel—103 (111, 119, 127, 135) sts total.

Under Collar

Knit 1 (WS) row. Cont in St st, work even until collar measures 1¾" (4.5 cm), ending with a WS row. Shape under-collar as foll:

Row 1: Knit to last 5 sts, turn.

Row 2: Yo, purl to last 5 sts, turn.

Row 3: Yo, knit to 6 sts before gap, turn.

Row 4: Yo, purl to 6 sts before gap, turn.

Rep the last 2 rows 3 more times. Work 3 rows even, closing gaps as you come to them. Knit 1 (WS) row for turning ridge.

Top of Collar

Shape top of collar as foll:

Row 1: Knit to last 25 sts, turn.

Row 2: Yo, purl to last 25 sts, turn.

Row 3: Yo, knit to 1 st before gap, k2tog, k4, turn.

Row 4: Yo, purl to 1 st before gap, ssp, p4, turn.

Rep Rows 3 and 4 until all sts have been worked. Cont even in St st until top of collar is 2 rows longer than under collar. BO all sts.

Fold lapels, facings, and hems to WS. With MC threaded on a tapestry needle, sew in place, allowing sufficient ease for lapels to fold back. Fold collar to WS and sew into place as for lapels.

Fasten the jacket with a leather belt instead of buttons.

A simple four-stitch, four-row Fair Isle pattern decorates much of **Shirley Paden's** warm shawl-collar jacket. She worked the background stitches in off-white throughout, but changed the color of the pattern stitches in wide bands. She added a large star motif, which shades from dark to light to dark again, as a focal point along the lower body and sleeves. The jacket fastens with an I-cord belt threaded through eyelets at the waist. Colorful pom-poms finish off the ends of the belt and prevent it from inadvertently slipping out of the eyelets. To maintain the clean lines of the silhouette, Shirley trimmed the edges with I-cord.

NOTES

✤ A garter-stitch selvedge is worked at each selvedge edge. Work all increases and decreases inside these selvedge stitches.

✤ The number of rows to be worked is provided for each color change so that the flow of color from bottom to top is consistent.

STITCH GUIDE

Sloped Cast-On

(Used for shaping collar) Add stitches at the end of right-side rows for purl side increases and at the end of wrong-side rows for knit side increases as follows: Using the backward-loop method (see Glossary, page 133), cast on the specified number of sts, then turn work. On purl rows: Holding the yarn in front with enough tension to prevent the last CO st from slipping off, slip the first st from the left needle to the right needle purlwise, purl the next stitch through the back loop (tbl). On knit rows: Holding the yarn in back with enough tension to prevent the last CO st from slipping off, slip the first st from the left needle to the right needle as if to purl tbl, knit the second st through the back loop.

FINISHED SIZE

35 (46½)" (89 [118] cm) bust circumference, fastened. To fit bust sizes 31–34 (36–44)" (79–87 [92–112] cm). Cardigan shown measures 35" (89 cm). **Note:** Due to the large number of stitches in the star motif, only two sizes are provided.

YARN

Worsted weight (#4 Medium).

Shown here: Classic Elite Montera (50% llama, 50% wool; 127 yd [116 m]/100 g): #3845 fieldstone heather (ecru; MC), 7 (9) skeins; #3833 honeybell (orange), #3885 bolsita orange (burnt orange), #3868 ancient orange (rust), and #3827 cochineal (plum), 1 skein each.

NEEDLES

Body and sleeves—size U.S.10 (6 mm). Collar and I-cord—size U.S. 9 (5.5 mm): straight and set of 2 double-pointed (dpn). Edging—size U.S. 8 (5 mm): 32" (80 cm) circular (cir). Adjust needle size if necessary to obtain the correct gauge.

NOTIONS

Marker (m); tapestry needle; waste yarn; stitch holders; three white hook-and-eye closures (available at fabric stores); sharp-point sewing needle and matching thread.

GAUGE

19 stitches and 21 rows = 4" (10 cm) according to Diamond Seeding chart or Star chart on largest needles.

Sloped Bind-Off

Use this technique for the first st to be bound-off on any bind-off row to prevent the "stair steps" produced when working multiple bind-off sequences. Do not work the last st of the row before the bind-off row. With the yarn in back, slip the first st on the left needle purlwise to the right needle, then lift the unworked st up and over this st and off the needle. Work the rest of the bind-off on this row in the usual manner.

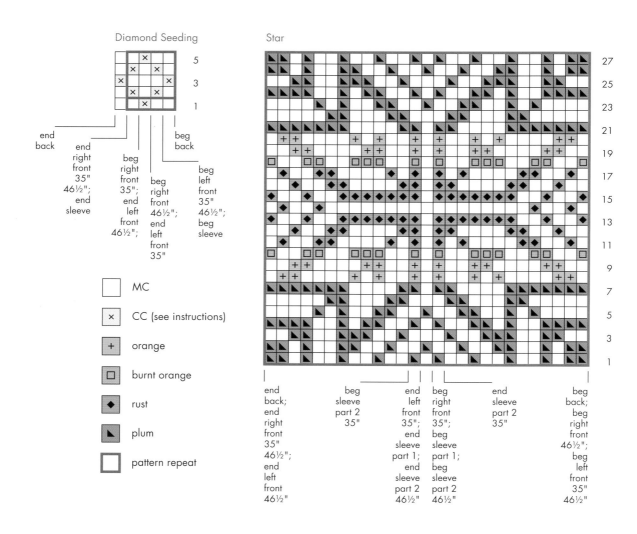

Diamond Seeding

end back

end right front 35" 46½"; end sleeve

end right front 35"; end left front 46½";

beg right front 46½"; end left front 35"

beg left front 35" 46½"; beg sleeve

beg back

MC

CC (see instructions)

orange

burnt orange

rust

plum

pattern repeat

Star

end back; end right front 35" 46½"; end left front 46½"

beg sleeve part 2 35"

end left front 35"; end sleeve part 1; end sleeve part 2 46½"

beg right front 35"; beg sleeve part 1; beg sleeve part 2 46½"

end sleeve part 2 35"

beg back; beg right front 46½"; beg left front 35" 46½"

BACK

With MC and largest needles, CO 83 (111) sts. *Next row:* (WS) K1 (selvedge st; knit every row), p81 (109), k1 (selvedge st; knit every row). Knitting the first and last st of every row as established for selvedge sts (see Notes), work Rows 1–5 of Diamond Seeding chart, using plum as CC. With MC, work 3 rows in St st, dec 0 (1) st on last row by working last 2 sts as k2 (k2tog)—83 (110) sts rem. Maintaining selvedge sts, work Rows 1–27 of Star chart. With MC, work 3 rows in St st, using the M1 method (see Glossary, page 137) to inc 0 (1) st before selvedge st at end of last row—83 (111) sts. Using plum as CC, work Rows 1–5 of Diamond Seeding chart—piece measures about 8½" (21.5 cm) from CO.

Waistband

With MC, work 2 rows in St st. Work eyelet row for your size as foll:

Size 35" only

K1 (selvedge st), p2, yo, p2tog, *p3, yo, p2tog; rep from * to last 3 sts, p2, k1 (selvedge st)—16 eyelets.

Size 46½" only

K1 (selvedge st), p4, yo, p2tog, [p5, yo, p2tog, p4, yo, p2tog] 7 times, p5, yo, p2tog, p5, k1 (selvedge st)—16 eyelets.

Both sizes

Work 2 rows in St st—piece measures about 9¼" (23.5 cm) from CO. Beg with Row 1, then rep Rows 2–5, work Diamond Seeding chart for a total of 32 rows, changing CC as foll: 5 rows plum, 12 rows burnt orange, 12 rows rust, and 3 rows orange—piece measures about 15½" (39.5 cm) from CO.

Use two (or more) colors to make pom-poms more interesting.

Shape Armholes

Note: The color patt changes on the last row of armhole shaping; read all the way through the foll instructions before proceeding. Cont in Diamond Seeding patt, working 9 (13) more rows with CC orange, and using the sloped bind-off technique (see Stitch Guide), BO 3 (4) sts at beg of next 2 rows, then BO 2 (3) sts at beg of foll 2 (4) rows, then BO 1 (2) st(s) at beg of foll 6 (4) rows, then BO 0 (1) st at beg of foll 0 (4) rows—67 (79) sts rem. *At the same time,* beg with the last row of armhole shaping (the 10th [14th] row), change CC to rust for 12 rows, then change CC to burnt orange for 17 rows—armholes measure about 7¼ (8)" (18.5 [20.5] cm). Change to middle-size needles and MC and k17 (21), BO center 33 (37) sts for neck, knit to end—17 (21) sts rem each side. Place sts on holders and cut yarn, leaving a tail long enough to work the three-needle BO later.

RIGHT FRONT

With MC and largest needles, CO 43 (56) sts. Knitting the first and last st of every row for selvedge sts, purl 1 (WS) row. With plum as CC and beg and end as indicated for your size, work Rows 1–5 of Diamond Seeding chart. With MC, work 3 rows in St st. Beg and end as indicated for your size, work Rows 1–27 of Star chart. With MC, work 3 rows in St st. With plum as CC and beg and end as indicated for your size, work Rows 1–5 of Diamond Seeding chart—piece measures same as back to waist.

Waistband

With MC, work 2 rows in St st. Work eyelet row for your size as foll:

Size 35" only

K1 (selvedge st), p2, yo, p2tog, *p3, yo, p2tog; rep from * to last 3 sts, p2, k1 (selvedge st)—8 eyelets.

Size 46½" only

K1 (selvedge st), [p4, yo, p2tog] 3 times, p5, yo, p2tog, p4, yo, p2tog, p5, yo, p2tog, [p4, yo, p2tog] 2 times, p4, k1 (selvedge st)—8 eyelets.

Both sizes

Work 2 rows in St st. Beg with Row 1, then rep Rows 2–5, work Diamond Seeding chart as before for a total of 70 (74) rows, changing CC as for back. *At the same time,* when 26 (30) rows of Diamond Seeding patt have been worked, shape V-neck and armhole as foll.

Shape V-Neck and Armhole

Note: The V-neck and armhole are shaped at the same time; read all the way through the foll section before proceeding. Cont in patt and using the sloped bind-off technique, BO 1 st at neck edge every other row 15 (17) times, then every 4th row 3 (2) times and *at the same time*, when 33 rows of Diamond Seeding patt have been worked, shape armhole as foll: BO 3 (4) sts at armhole edge once, then BO 2 (3) sts at armhole edge 1 (2) time(s), then BO 1 (2) st(s) at armhole edge 3 (2) times, then BO 0 (1) st at armhole edge 0 (2) times—17 (21) sts rem when all shaping is complete. Work even as established until piece measures same as back to shoulders, ending with 1 row MC as for back. Place sts on holders and cut yarn, leaving a tail long enough to work the three-needle BO later.

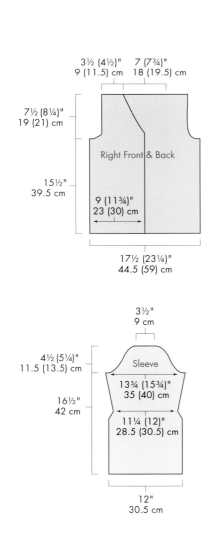

3½ (4½)" 7 (7¾)"
9 (11.5) cm 18 (19.5) cm

7½ (8¼)"
19 (21) cm

Right Front & Back

15½"
39.5 cm

9 (11¾)"
23 (30) cm

17½ (23¼)"
44.5 (59) cm

3½"
9 cm

4½ (5¼)"
11.5 (13.5) cm

Sleeve

13¾ (15¾)"
35 (40) cm

16½"
42 cm

11¼ (12)"
28.5 (30.5) cm

12"
30.5 cm

With careful planning, the color pattern on sleeve caps can match the pattern on a bodice.

LEFT FRONT

Work as for Right Front, reversing all shaping by beg V-neck shaping after 27 (31) rows of Diamond Seeding patt have been worked, and beg armhole shaping after 34 rows of Diamond Seeding patt have been worked.

SLEEVES

With MC and largest needles, CO 57 sts. Knitting the first and last st of every row for selvedge sts, purl 1 (WS) row. With plum as CC and beg and end as indicated for sleeve, work Rows 1–5 of Diamond Seeding chart. With MC, work 3 rows in St st. Beg and end as indicated for sleeve part 1, work Rows 1–27 of Star chart. With MC, work 3 rows in St st. With plum as CC and beg and end as indicated for sleeve, work Rows 1–5 of Diamond Seeding chart— piece measures about 8½" (21.5 cm) from CO. With MC, purl 1 row. Dec 4 (0) sts on next row as foll (decs are spaced to avoid distortion of diamond peaks):

Size 35" only
K1 (selvedge st), k7, k2tog, k10, k2tog, k13, k2tog, k10, k2tog, k7, k1 (selvedge st)—53 sts rem.

Size 46½" only
Knit 1 row.

Both sizes
Purl 1 row. Beg and end as indicated for your size for sleeve part 2, work Rows 12–16 of Star chart. With MC, work 3 rows in St st. Beg with plum and foll the color sequence used for the back, beg and end as indicated for sleeve, work Diamond Seeding chart for 32 rows and *at the same time* inc 1 st each end of needle on the first row of the chart, then every 4th (2nd) row 4 (3) times, then every 5th (3rd) row 1 (5) time(s)—65 (75) sts. After 32 rows of Diamond Seeding chart are complete and piece measures 16½" (42 cm) from CO, shape sleeve cap as foll.

Shape Cap

Cont in Diamond Seeding patt and color sequence as established, use the sloped bind-off technique to BO 4 sts at beg of next 2 rows, then BO 3 sts at beg of foll 2 (4) rows, then BO 2 sts at beg of foll 4 (6) rows—43 sts rem. *BO 1 st at beg of next 2 rows, then BO 2 sts at beg of foll 2 rows (6 sts BO in 4 rows). Rep from * 2 more times—25 sts rem. BO 4 sts at beg of next 2 rows—17 sts rem. *Next row:* (RS) With MC, sl 1, knit to end. With WS facing, BO all sts.

COLLAR

With MC and middle-size needles, CO 41 sts. Using the sloped cast-on technique (see Stitch Guide) and working in St st, CO 5 sts at the end of the next 4 rows, then CO 4 sts at the end of the foll 6 rows, then CO 3 sts at the end of the foll 8 rows—109 sts; 18 rows total. *Next row:* Using plum as CC, work Row 1 of Diamond Seeding chart as foll: K4 with MC, k1 with CC, *k3 with MC, k1 with CC; rep from * 24 more times, k4 with MC. *Next row:* (Row 2 of chart) P3 with MC, p1 with CC, *p1 with MC, p1 with CC; rep from * 50 more times, p3 with MC. *Next row:* (Row 3 of chart) K2 with MC, k1 with CC, *k3 with MC, k1 with CC; rep from * 25 more times, k2 with MC. *Next row:* (Row 4 of chart) P3 with MC, p1 with CC, *p1 with MC, p1 with CC; rep from * 50 more times, p3 with MC.

Shape Back Neck

(Row 5 of chart) Using the sloped bind-off technique, BO 2 sts (1 st on right needle), cont as foll: k1 with MC, k1 with CC, *k3 with MC, k1 with CC; rep from * 24 more times, k4 with MC—107 sts rem. Change to MC and, using the sloped bind-off technique, BO 2 sts at beg of next row, then BO 4 sts at beg of foll 2 rows, then BO 2 sts at beg of foll 2 rows, then BO 4 sts at beg of foll 4 rows, then BO 6 sts at beg of foll 6 rows—41 sts rem. BO all sts.

BELT (I-CORD)

With MC and middle-size dpn, CO 3 sts. Work 3-st I-cord as foll: *K3, do not turn, slide these 3 sts to opposite needle tip, bring yarn around back and rep from *. Work in this manner until piece measures 55" (139.5 cm), or desired length. (*Note:* Belt shown is designed to reach lower edge of cardigan when tied into a bow.) Cut yarn, thread tail on a tapestry needle and draw it through the 3 sts in the same order that they were knitted, pull tight, and secure them by taking a small st. Pull yarn through to the center of the cord to hide the end.

Use the stranded technique of carrying the unused yarn across the back of the knitted stitches to create a fabric that's twice as warm.

FINISHING

Weave in loose ends. Block pieces to measurements. Using the three-needle method (see Glossary, page 133), join fronts to back at shoulders, using the tails already attached. With MC threaded on a tapestry needle, sew side seams.

Collar

With RS of collar facing WS of garment, pin collar to neckline, aligning the center of the collar with the center back neck. With MC threaded on a tapestry needle, use a whipstitch (see Glossary, page 139) to sew it in place. Collar will fold back so RS will be visible when worn.

Sleeve Edging

With MC, middle-size needle, and WS facing, pick up and purl (see Glossary, page 138) 48 sts evenly spaced across lower cuff edge, then use the cable method (see Glossary, page 133) to CO 3 more sts—51 sts total. Work attached I-cord as foll: *K2, sl 1 kwise, knit the last picked-up st, then psso. Slip the 3 sts back to the left needle. Rep from * until all picked-up sts have been used—3 CO sts rem. Cut yarn, leaving a tail about 10" (25.5 cm) long. Secure the rem 3 sts as for the belt. Sew the ends of the edging tog, then sew sleeve seam to beg of cap shaping.

Front and Collar Edging

With MC, smallest cir needle, WS facing, and beg at lower left front edge, pick up and purl 50 (52) sts evenly spaced to beg of collar, picking up just inside the selvedge sts. Thread a length of waste yarn onto a tapestry needle and carefully transfer the sts onto the waste yarn. Using the knitted method, pick up and knit 100 sts across the RS of the collar, then transfer these sts to a second length of waste yarn. With WS facing, pick up and purl 50 (52) sts along right front edge, picking up last st in the CO edge—200 (204) sts total. Using the cable method, CO 3 sts at the end of this needle. With middle-size dpn, work attached I-cord as for sleeve edging to the top of the right front, slip the last 3 sts onto a holder, slip the held collar sts onto smaller cir needle, then slip the 3 held sts back onto the same needle. Cont working attached I-cord across collar (*Note:* WS of collar will be facing). When only 3 sts rem, slip these sts onto a holder, transfer the held left front sts onto needle, then slip the 3 held sts back onto the same needle. Cont working attached I-cord until only 3 sts rem. Secure the rem 3 sts as for the belt.

Lower Body Edging

With MC, smallest cir needle, WS facing, and beg at the center of the I-cord edging at lower right front, pick up and purl 36 (48) sts across right front, 71 (98) sts across back, and 36 (48) sts across left front, picking up last st in the center of the left front I-cord—143 (194) sts total. Using the cable method, CO 3 sts at the end of this needle. Work attached I-cord edging as for the front and collar. Secure rem 3 sts as for the belt.

With MC threaded on a tapestry needle and RS of collar facing, use a whipstitch to secure I-cord edging around front of collar. Sew sleeve caps into armholes, matching colors. With sharp-point sewing needle and matching thread, sew 3 sets of hooks and eyes to fronts, placing the highest at the base of the V-neck, and the others at 1½" (3.8 cm) intervals below that. Beg and ending at center front, thread belt through waist eyelets. Make two 2" (5 cm) pom-poms (see Glossary, page 138), using 50 wraps of burnt orange and 25 wraps of orange for each pom-pom. Sew a pom-pom to each end of belt.

For her warm, richly patterned gloves, **Véronik Avery** combined oatmeal and gray in several Fair Isle patterns, beginning with corrugated ribbing followed by a narrow band that spells out "peace" on the right glove and "love" on the left. The hands are worked in a houndstooth check and the thumb gussets use a salt-and-pepper pattern that alternates one stitch of each color. The thumbs and fingers are worked in a single color (no stranding) for digit flexibility. In addition to being knitted on small needles for tight, cold-resistant stitches, the yarn floats add a layer of warmth. A bit of bright embroidery on the back of the left hand livens up the muted colorway.

FINISHED SIZE
About 7¼" (18.5 cm) hand circumference and 10½" (26.5 cm) total length. To fit a woman's medium hand.

YARN
Fingering weight (#1 Super Fine).
Shown here: Reynolds Whiskey (100% wool; 195 yd [178 m]/50 g): #59 charcoal (MC), 2 balls; #31 silver (CC), 1 ball.

NEEDLES
Size U.S. 0 (2 mm): set of 5 double-pointed (dpn). Adjust needle size if necessary to obtain the correct gauge.

NOTIONS
Markers (m); waste yarn or stitch holders; tapestry needle; one skein each of Paternayan Persian yarn (available at needlepoint stores) in #953 strawberry, #840 salmon, #676 green apple, and #752 old gold for embroidery.

GAUGE
20 stitches and 18 rounds = 2" (5 cm) in colorwork pattern, worked in rounds.

NOTE
✦ When picking up stitches at the base of the fingers, simply insert the needle into the stitches without knitting them; i.e., do not pick up and knit.

RIGHT GLOVE
With MC, CO 64 sts. Distribute sts evenly onto 4 dpn, place marker (pm) and join for working in rnds, being careful not to twist sts. Join CC, *k2 with MC, k2 with CC; rep from * to end of rnd.

Cuff
*K2 with MC, p2 with CC; rep from * to end. Cont in rib as established until piece measures 1½" (3.8 cm) from CO. With MC, knit 2 rnds. Work Rnds 1–9 of Peace chart. With MC, knit 2 rnds, inc 4 sts evenly spaced on last rnd—68 sts.

Thumb Gusset
K1 with MC, work Row 1 of Hand chart across next 40 sts, pm, work Row 1 of Thumb Gusset chart across next 3 sts, pm, work last 24 sts according to Hand chart. Working the first st in MC, cont as established through Row 19 of Thumb Gusset chart—21 gusset sts between markers. Cont in patts as established until thumb gusset measures 3" (7.5 cm).

Peace

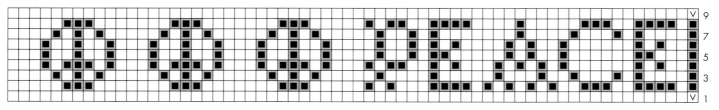

Love

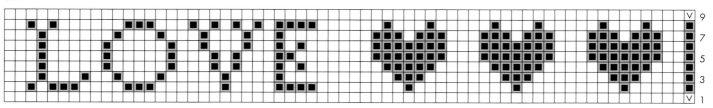

Thumb Gusset

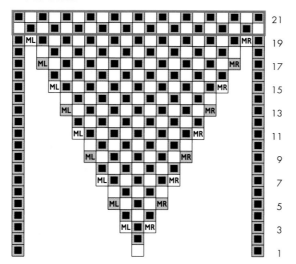

Hand

		with MC, knit
		with CC, knit
V		sl 1 wyb
MR		with MC, M1R
ML		with MC, M1L
MR		with CC, M1R
ML		with CC, M1L
		pattern repeat

Upper Palm

Work in patt as established to gusset marker, place 21 gusset sts onto waste yarn or stitch holder, use the backward-loop method (see Glossary, page 133) to CO 8 sts over gap, rejoin, and knit to end—73 sts. Work even in established patt, working new sts according to Hand chart, until piece measures 1½" (3.8 cm) from thumb gusset.

Little Finger

With MC, k10, place next 54 sts on waste yarn or holder (for back of hand and palm), use the backward-loop method to CO 4 sts, k9—23 sts. *Next rnd*: K9, ssk, k2, k2tog, knit to end—21 sts rem. Work even until finger measures 2" (5 cm) or ¼" (6 mm) less than desired total length. Dec for tip as foll:

Rnd 1: *K2tog; rep from * to last st, k1—11 sts rem.
Rnd 2: *K2tog; rep from * to last st, k1—6 sts rem.

Cut yarn, thread tail through rem sts, pull tight to close hole, and secure to WS.

Replace 54 held sts on needles; pick up 2 sts at base of little finger (do not pick up and knit; see Note) and transfer to left needle; reattach MC and k1, k2tog, knit to last st, sl last st to right needle, pick up 2 more sts at base of little finger and transfer to left needle, then replace slipped st onto left needle, ssk, k1—56 sts. Pm and rejoin for working in rnds. Knit 4 rnds.

Feel free to combine several different Fair Isle patterns.

Ring Finger

K10, place next 36 sts on holder for back of hand and palm, use the backward-loop method to CO 4 sts, k10—24 sts. *Next rnd:* K9, ssk, k2, k2tog, knit to end—22 sts rem. Work even until finger measures about 2½" (6.5 cm) or ¼" (6 mm) less than desired total length. Dec for tip as foll:

Rnd 1: *K2tog; rep from * to end—11 sts rem.

Rnd 2: *K2tog; rep from * to last st, k1—6 sts rem.

Cut yarn, thread tail through rem sts, pull tight to close hole, and secure to WS.

Middle Finger

Replace next 9 held sts (back of hand) onto needles, rejoin MC, knit these 9 sts, CO 4 sts as before, replace last 9 held sts (palm) onto dpn, knit these 9 sts, then pick up 4 sts (see Note) along base of ring finger with left needle—26 sts. Knit first 2 picked-up sts, then pm for beg of rnd. *Next rnd:* *K1, k2tog, k7, ssk, k1; rep from * once more—22 sts rem. Work even until finger measures about 2¾" (7 cm) or ¼" (6 mm) less than desired total length. Decrease tip and finish as for ring finger.

Index Finger

Replace rem 18 held sts onto needles, then pick up 4 sts (see Note) along base of middle finger, placing first 2 picked-up sts onto right needle and last 2 picked-up sts onto left needle—22 sts. Pm for beg of rnd between the 4 picked-up sts. Rejoin MC. *Next rnd:* K1, k2tog, knit to last 3 sts, ssk, k1—20 sts rem. Work even until finger measures about 2" (5 cm) or ¼" (6 mm) less than desired total length. Dec for tip as foll:

Rnd 1: *K2tog; rep from * to end—10 sts rem.

Rnd 2: *K2tog; rep from * to end—5 sts rem.

Cut yarn, thread tail through rem sts, pull tight to close hole, and secure to WS.

Thumb

Replace 21 held gusset sts onto dpn, then pick up 8 sts (see Note) along upper palm, placing first 4 picked-up sts onto right needle and last 4 picked-up sts onto left needle—29 sts. Pm for beg of rnd between the 8 picked-up sts. Rejoin MC.

Rnd 1: K3, k2tog, knit to last 5 sts, ssk, k3—27 sts rem.

Rnd 2: K2, k2tog, knit to last 4 sts, ssk, k2—25 sts rem.

Work even until thumb measures 2" (5 cm) or ¼" (6 mm) less than desired total length. Dec for tip:

Rnd 1: *K2tog; rep from * to last st, k1—13 sts rem.

Rnd 2: *K2tog; rep from * to last st, k1—7 sts rem.

Cut yarn, thread tail through rem sts, pull tight to close hole, and secure to WS.

Just a touch of embroidery can have a big effect.

LEFT GLOVE

With MC, CO 64 sts. Distribute sts evenly onto 4 dpn, place marker (pm) and join for working in rnds, being careful not to twist sts. Join CC, *k2 with MC, k2 with CC; rep from * to end of rnd. Work cuff as for right hand, substituting Love chart for Peace chart.

Thumb Gusset

Knit 1 MC, work Row 1 of Hand chart across next 24 sts, pm, work Row 1 of Thumb Gusset chart across next 3 sts, pm, work across last 40 sts according to Hand chart. Cont as for right hand.

FINISHING

Weave in loose ends. With a single strand of Persian yarn threaded on a tapestry needle, use the stem st and straight st to embroider (see Glossary, pages 135–136, for embroidery instructions) flower on back of left hand as shown in illustration at right. Block lightly.

Embroider a four-petal flower on the back of the left hand.

RETRO ANDEAN PULLOVER
MARY JANE MUCKLESTONE

Inspired by the colorful earflap hats worn in the high Andes, **Mary Jane Mucklestone** combined bright stripes, geometric patterns, and animal motifs in this alpaca pullover. The body is worked in rounds from the lower edge to the shoulders and decorated with Fair Isle motifs and simple narrow stripes along the way. The sleeves, too, are worked in rounds to the armholes, then the caps are shaped in rows and the figures worked in a combination of intarsia and Fair Isle.

STITCH GUIDE

Main Stripe Sequence
2 rnds each in MC, turquoise, green, white, red, orange, and pink—14 rnds total.

Shoulder Stripe Sequence
2 rnds each in turquoise, green, orange, and pink—8 rnds total.

NOTES

✦ The sweater body is worked in the round to underarms, then steeks are added for the armholes and neck, and the body is continued in the round to the shoulders.

✦ Work the isolated motifs on the sleeve caps in a combination of intarsia and Fair Isle, using a separate strand of white for the motif, carrying the main color across the back of the motif, and twisting yarns around each other at the beginning and end of the motif.

FINISHED SIZE
About 28¼ (37¾, 47¼, 56¾)" (72 [96, 120, 144] cm) bust circumference. Sweater shown measures 28¼" (72 cm).

YARN
Worsted weight (#4 Medium).
Shown here: Classic Elite Inca Alpaca (100% alpaca; 109 yd [100 m]/50 g): #1129 Lincoln blue (MC), 4 (5, 7, 8) skeins; #1116 natural (white), 2 (3, 5, 6) skeins; #1125 aqua spray (turquoise), #1111 peridot (green), #1130 dahlia (red), #1151 tulip (pink), and #1183 oriole (orange), 1 (1, 2, 2) skein(s) each.

NEEDLES
Sizes U.S. 5, 6, and 7 (3.75, 4, and 4.5 mm): 24" (60 cm) circular (cir) and set of 4 or 5 double-pointed (dpn). Adjust needle size if necessary to obtain the correct gauge.

NOTIONS
Markers (m); stitch holders; tapestry needle; sewing machine or sharp-point sewing needle; matching thread.

GAUGE
22 stitches and 22 rounds = 4" (10 cm) in Fair Isle color pattern on largest needle, worked in rounds; 22 stitches and 28 rounds = 4" (10 cm) in St st on middle-size needle, worked in rounds.

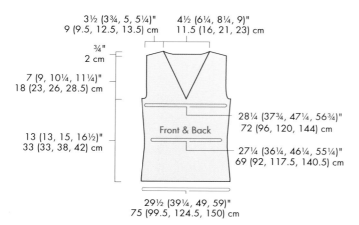

3½ (3¾, 5, 5¼)"
9 (9.5, 12.5, 13.5) cm

4½ (6¼, 8¼, 9)"
11.5 (16, 21, 23) cm

¾"
2 cm

7 (9, 10¼, 11¼)"
18 (23, 26, 28.5) cm

Front & Back

28¼ (37¾, 47¼, 56¾)"
72 (96, 120, 144) cm

13 (13, 15, 16½)"
33 (33, 38, 42) cm

27¼ (36¼, 46¼, 55¼)"
69 (92, 117.5, 140.5) cm

29½ (39¼, 49, 59)"
75 (99.5, 124.5, 150) cm

4¾ (5¾, 7, 7¾)"
12 (14.5, 18, 19.5) cm

Sleeve

12 (16, 19¼, 21)"
30.5 (40.5, 49, 53.5) cm

19"
48.5 cm

8¾ (10¼, 11¾, 11¾)"
22 (26, 30, 30) cm

BODY

With MC and smallest needle, CO 150 (200, 250, 300) sts, placing a marker (pm) after the 75 (100, 125, 150)th st to mark right side "seam." Pm to mark end of rnd and left side seam, and join for working in rnds, being careful not to twist sts. Work in k1, p1 rib until piece measures 1¾" (4.5 cm) from CO, and inc 12 (16, 20, 24) sts evenly spaced on last rnd—162 (216, 270, 324) sts. Change to largest needle and work Rnds 1–12 of Chevron chart. Change to middle-size needle. Cont in St st (knit every rnd), work main stripe sequence (see Stitch Guide) 2 (2, 3, 3) times, then work 1 rnd with MC and *at the same time* dec 1 st each side of each m every 4th rnd 3 (4, 4, 5) times, then inc 1 st each side of each m every 4th rnd 1 time—154 (204, 258, 308) sts. Work 1 more rnd with MC, dec 0 (1, 0, 0) st on front and inc 0 (0, 1, 0) st on back—154 (203, 259, 308) sts. Change to largest needle and work Rnds 1–7 of Zig-Zag chart. Change to middle-size needle and knit 2 rnds with white, inc 0 (2, 0, 1) st(s) on front and inc 2 (3, 1, 3) st(s) on back on second rnd—156 (208, 260, 312) sts; 77 (103, 129, 155) sts for front and 79 (105, 131, 157) sts for back. Knit 2 rnds with MC. Change to largest needle and work Rnds 1–12 of Bird chart. Change to middle-size needle and work 2 rnds with MC, then work main stripe sequence in reverse order 2 (3, 4, 4) times and *at the same time*, when piece measures 13 (13, 15, 16½)" (33 [33, 38, 42] cm) from CO, ending 4 sts before end of rnd, shape armholes and neck as foll.

Shape Armholes and Neck

BO next 8 sts, removing m, work to 4 sts before next m, BO next 8 sts, knit to end—69 (95, 121, 147) sts rem for front and 71 (97, 123, 149) sts rem for back. Pm, CO 7 sts over left armhole gap for steek, pm for beg of rnd, work across front sts, pm, CO 7 sts over right armhole gap for steek, pm, work to end of rnd—154 (206, 258, 310) sts total, including steek sts. Work steek sts in St st, alternating 1 st in each color on two-color rnds. Mark center front st. *Note:* The arm-

Bird

Chevron

Boy

Girl

Zig-Zag

Triangle

✕	MC
•	white
☐	pattern repeat

holes and neck are shaped at the same time; read all the way through the foll section before proceeding. Cont in patt, dec 1 st at each armhole edge every other rnd 4 (10, 12, 21) times and *at the same time*, on second dec rnd, place neck steek as foll: Work to marked center st, place center st on holder, pm, CO 7 sts for neck steek, pm, work to end of rnd—152 (204, 256, 308) sts, including all steek sts. Dec 1 st at each neck edge every other rnd 6 (9, 14, 15) times, then every 4th rnd 5 (7, 7, 8) times—122 (140, 174, 186) sts rem. *At the same time*, after armhole shaping and stripe sequence are complete, pm 5 (6, 9, 10) sts from left front armhole edge for Boy chart, 14 (15, 18, 19) sts from right front armhole edge for Girl chart, and 2 (4, 5, 4) sts from right back armhole edge for back charts. With MC, work until armhole measures 4½ (6½, 7¾, 8¾)" (11.5 [16.5, 19.5, 22] cm). *Next rnd:* Work to first chart m, work Row 1 of Boy chart, work to next chart m, work Row 1 of Girl chart, work to back chart m, *work Row 1 of Boy chart, work 1 st with MC, work Row 1 of Girl chart, work 1 st with MC; rep from * 2 (2, 3, 4) more times, work Row 1 of Boy chart 0 (1, 1, 0) more time, work to end of rnd. Cont through Row 13 of each chart, then work 1 rnd with MC only. *Next rnd:* With MC, work to right armhole steek, BO 7 steek sts, work to left armhole steek, BO 7 steek sts—45 (49, 61, 65) sts rem for front (including 7 steek sts) and 63 (77, 99, 107) sts rem for back. Place back sts on a holder.

Shape Front Shoulders

Working back and forth in rows and working first 6 rows of shoulder stripe sequence (see Stitch Guide), BO 7 (7, 9, 10) sts at beg of next 2 (6, 6, 4) rows, then BO 6 (0, 0, 9) sts at beg of foll 4 (0, 0, 2) rows—7 steek sts rem. With same color, BO steek sts.

Shape Back Shoulders

Return 63 (77, 99, 107) back sts to needle. With RS facing, join turquoise. Working in shoulder stripe sequence, BO 7 (7, 9, 10) sts at beg of next 2 (6, 6, 4) rows, then BO 6 (0, 0, 9) sts at beg of foll 4 (0, 0, 2) rows—25 (35, 45, 49) sts rem. Work 1 row even. BO all sts.

SLEEVES

With MC and smallest dpn, CO 46 (54, 62, 62) sts. Pm and join for working in rnds, being careful not to twist sts. Work in k1, p1 rib until piece measures 3" (7.5 cm) from CO, inc 2 sts evenly spaced in last rnd—48 (56, 64, 64) sts. With MC and middle-size needles, knit 1 rnd. Change to largest dpn and work Rows 1–7 of Triangle chart. *Note:* Increases are introduced while the color pattern changes; there may not be enough sts to work a full rep of a chart; read all the way through the next section before proceeding. Change to middle-size dpn and work main stripe sequence 2 times, work 2 rnds with MC, change to largest dpn and work Rows 1–7 of Zig-Zag chart, change to middle-size dpn and work main stripe sequence 2 more times, work 2 rnds with MC, change to largest dpn and work Rows 1–12 of Bird chart, change

Stripes, color stranding (Fair Isle), and intarsia— this sweater has it all!

to middle-size dpn and work 2 rnds with MC, work 14 rnds of main stripe sequence in reverse order, work in MC until piece measures about 19" (48.5 cm) from CO and *at the same time* inc 1 st each side of marker on first rnd, then every 8th (6th, 4th, 3rd) rnd 8 (15, 20, 25) more times—66 (88, 106, 116) sts.

Shape Cap
With MC, BO 3 sts at beg of next rnd—63 (85, 103, 113) sts rem. Working back and forth in rows, BO 4 sts at beg of next row—59 (81, 99, 109) sts rem. Mark center 9 sts. *Next row:* (RS) BO 2 sts, knit to marked sts, work Row 1 of Boy chart for right sleeve or Girl chart for left sleeve, knit to end—57 (79, 97, 107) sts rem. *Next row:* BO 2 sts, work as established to end—55 (77, 95, 105) sts rem. Cont in patt, changing to MC after chart is complete, dec 1 st each end of needle every RS row 9 (10, 13, 14) times—37 (57, 69, 77) sts rem. Dec 1 st each end of needle every row 5 (9, 12, 15) times—27 (39, 45, 47) sts rem. BO 5 sts at beg of next 4 rows—7 (19, 25, 27) sts rem. BO all sts.

FINISHING
Steam-block thoroughly.

Cut Steeks
See page 126 for finishing steeks. Machine stitch (or handstitch with sewing needle and thread) two lines of closely spaced sts on each side of center of armhole and neck steeks. Carefully cut between lines of sts on each steek.

Weave in loose ends, following like colors on WS when possible. With MC threaded on a tapestry needle, sew front to back at shoulders. Sew sleeve caps into armholes between steek and body.

Neckband
Mark center front st. With MC, smallest cir needle, RS facing, and beg at left shoulder seam, pick up and knit 46 (58, 66, 72) sts along left front neck edge between steek and body, k1 held center st, pick up and knit 46 (58, 66, 72) sts along right front neck edge and 25 (35, 45, 49) sts across back neck—118 (152, 178, 194) sts total. Pm and join for working in rnds. Work in k1, p1 rib for 5 rnds and *at the same time* work a double dec at center front every rnd as foll: work to 1 st before marked center st, sl 2 tog kwise, k1, p2sso. BO all sts.

Work color-stranding (Fair Isle) patterns in areas that are worked in rounds; work intarsia patterns for areas that are worked back and forth in rows.

In a twist on classic argyle patterning, **Ann Budd** worked colorful diamonds in different sizes against a neutral background on the front of this lightweight vest. She chose different colors to accent the diagonal lines. Because a different "ball" of yarn is needed for each color area, the same number of balls is used whether all the diamonds and diagonal lines are worked in the same color or not—and more colors are so much more fun! A soft tweed yarn and round neck give the vest a casual look, and knit-three-purl-one ribs along the sides and across the back give it a slightly slimming fit while preventing the edges from curling.

FINISHED SIZE
About 33½ (36, 41, 46½)" (85 [91.5, 104, 118] cm) bust circumference. Vest shown measures 36" (91.5 cm).

YARN
Sportweight (#2 Fine).

Shown here: Rowan Felted Tweed (50% merino, 25% alpaca, 25% viscose; 191 yd [175 m]/50 g): #SH157 camel (tan; MC), 3 (4, 5, 6) balls; #SH158 pine (dark green; A), #SH154 ginger (rust; B), #SH150 rage (red; C), #SH161 avocado (light green; D), and #SH152 watery (teal; E), 1 ball each.

NEEDLES
Front and back—size 5 (3.75 cm). Neck and armbands—size 4 (3.5 mm): 16" (40 cm) circular (cir). Adjust needle size if necessary to obtain the correct gauge.

NOTIONS
Markers (m); bobbins for winding lengths of yarn (optional); tapestry needle.

GAUGE
24 stitches and 38 rows = 4" (10 cm) in stockinette stitch on larger needles.

NOTES

✤ Knit the first and last stitch of every row for selvedge stitches.

✤ Pay close attention to the chart—while the patterns for the diagonal lines and large diamonds begin on right-side rows, the patterns for the small diamonds begin on wrong-side rows.

✤ Work the Argyle chart in the intarsia method (see Design Notebook), using a separate ball or bobbin of yarn for each color block and twisting yarns around each other at color changes to prevent holes from forming.

BACK

With MC and larger needles, CO 102 (110, 126, 142) sts. *Set-up rib:* (RS) K1 (selvedge st; knit every row), *k2, p1, k1; rep from * to last st, k1 (selvedge st; knit every row). Maintaining selvedge sts, cont in rib on center 100 (108, 124, 140) sts as established (knit the knits and purl the purls) until piece measures 11 (11½, 12, 13)" (28 [29, 30.5, 33] cm) from CO, ending with a WS row.

Shape Armholes

Keeping in patt, BO 4 sts at beg of next 2 rows, then BO 3 sts at beg of foll 2 rows, then BO 2 sts at beg of foll 2 rows—84 (92, 108, 124) sts rem. Dec 1 st each end of needle every RS row 3 (4, 5, 7) times—78 (84, 98, 110) sts rem. Cont even in patt until armholes measure 8 (9, 9½, 11)" (20.5 [23, 24, 28] cm), ending with a WS row.

Shape Shoulders

BO 6 (7, 9, 10) sts at beg of next 6 (4, 4, 6) rows, then BO 0 (6, 8, 0) sts at beg of foll 0 (2, 2, 0) rows—42 (44, 46, 50) sts rem. BO all sts.

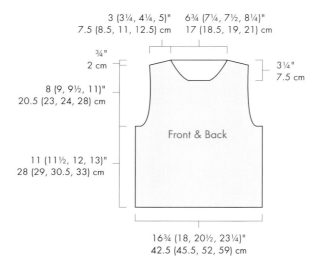

3 (3¼, 4¼, 5)"
7.5 (8.5, 11, 12.5) cm

6¾ (7¼, 7½, 8¼)"
17 (18.5, 19, 21) cm

¾"
2 cm

3¼"
7.5 cm

8 (9, 9½, 11)"
20.5 (23, 24, 28) cm

Front & Back

11 (11½, 12, 13)"
28 (29, 30.5, 33) cm

16¾ (18, 20½, 23¼)"
42.5 (45.5, 52, 59) cm

FRONT

With MC and larger needles, CO 102 (110, 126, 142) sts. *Set-up rib:* (RS) K1 (selvedge st; knit every row), *k2, p1, k1; rep from * to last st, k1 (selvedge st; knit every row). Maintaining selvedge sts, cont in rib on center 100 (108, 124, 140) sts as established until piece measures ¾" (2 cm) from CO, ending with a WS row. *Set-up body:* (RS) K1 (selvedge st), k2, p1, [k3, p1] 0 (1, 3, 5) time(s), k1, place marker (pm), k92 and *at the same time* inc 1 st to make a total of 93 sts, pm, k2, [p1, k3] 0 (1, 3, 5) time(s), p1, k1, k1 (selvedge st)—103 (111, 127, 143) sts. Maintaining selvedge sts, cont as established on center 101 (109, 125, 141) sts (knit the knits and purl the purls) until piece measures 6½ (7, 7½, 8½)" (16.5 [18, 19, 21.5] cm) from CO, ending with a WS row. *Next row:* (RS) Work to first m as established, work Row 1 of Argyle chart over next 93 sts to next m, work to end as established. Cont in this manner, foll chart on center 93 sts until piece measures same as back to armhole, ending with a WS row.

Work knit-three-purl-one ribs to gently draw in the back and sides.

Argyle

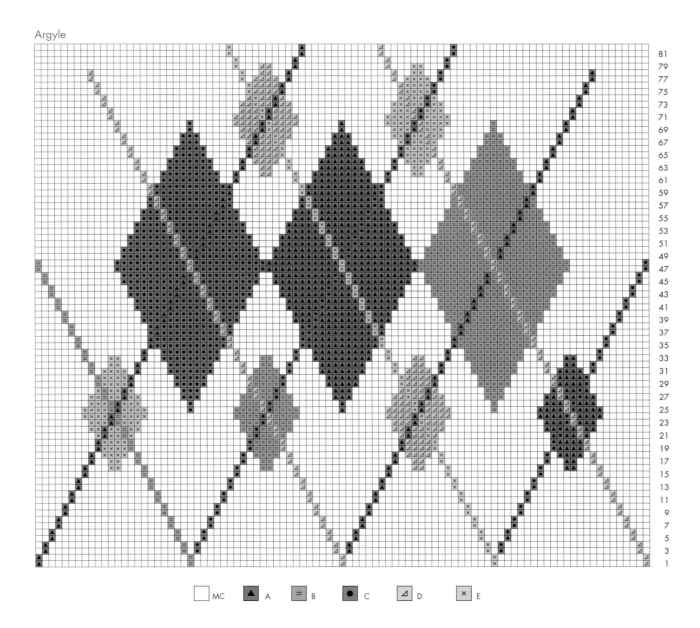

Mix up the colors and sizes of the argyle diamonds for a more interesting pattern.

Shape Armholes

Keeping in patt, BO 4 sts at beg of next 2 rows, then BO 3 sts at beg of foll 2 rows, then BO 2 sts at beg of foll 2 rows—85 (93, 109, 125) sts rem. Dec 1 st each end of needle every RS row 3 (4, 5, 7) times, removing markers when they are no longer needed—79 (85, 99, 111) sts rem. Cont even in patt until armholes measure 5½ (6½, 7, 8½)" (14 [16.5, 18, 21.5] cm), changing to MC when Row 82 of chart has been completed, ending with a WS row.

Shape Neck

Keeping in patt, work across 28 (30, 36, 40) sts, join a new ball of yarn and BO center 23 (25, 27, 31) sts, work to end—28 (30, 36, 40) sts rem each side. Working each side separately, at each neck edge BO 3 sts once, then BO 2 sts once, then dec 1 st every RS row 5 times—18 (20, 26, 30) sts rem each side. Cont even in St st until armholes measure same as back to beg of shoulder shaping.

Shape Shoulders

At each armhole edge, BO 6 (7, 9, 10) sts 3 (2, 2, 3) times, then BO rem 0 (6, 8, 0) sts.

FINISHING

Weave in loose ends, following along WS of like colors when possible. Block pieces to measurements. With MC threaded on a tapestry needle, sew front to back at shoulders. Sew side seams.

Neckband

With MC, smaller cir needle, RS facing, and beg at right shoulder seam, pick up and knit 42 (44, 46, 50) sts across back neck, 27 sts along left front neck edge, 23 (25, 27, 31) sts across front neck, and 28 sts along right front neck edge—120 (124, 128, 136) sts total. Pm and join for working in rnds. Work in k3, p1 rib until band measures ¾" (2 cm) from pick-up rnd. Loosely BO all sts in patt.

Armbands

With MC, smaller cir needle, RS facing, and beg at side seam, pick up and knit 116 (132, 140, 160) sts evenly spaced around armhole. Pm and join for working in rnds. Work in k3, p1 rib until band measures ¾" (2 cm) from pick-up rnd. Loosely BO all sts in patt. Lightly block again.

Intarsia allows for
color patterning without
adding bulk.

Intrigued by knitting's painterly possibilities, **Marta McCall** often turns to intarsia and felting for her designs. For the floral motif on this pillow, she gathered inspiration from printed ethnic fabrics. Marta knitted the pillow front in red wool with green and blue blocks for the foundations of the petal and leaf motifs. Then she felted the fabric and smoothed out the jagged boundaries between the color blocks by needlefelting lengths of yarn around the intarsia motifs. More needlefelting added isolated specks of orange within the petals and leaves. The felted piece is sewn to coordinating woven fabric and stuffed with polyester fiberfill. A fabric-covered cord covers the seams and gives the pillow a clean finish.

NOTES

✤ The pillow front is knitted with two strands of yarn held together; the pillow back is sewn from commercial fabric in a coordinating color.

✤ After the piece is knitted, it is felted in the washing machine, then once dry, additional colors are added with needlefelting.

✤ The barbs on the tip of the needlefelting needle are very sharp; work over a foam pad and take care not to pierce your fingers.

FINISHED SIZE
About 16" (40.5 cm) wide and 15" (38 cm) high, after felting.

YARN
Chunky weight (#5 Bulky).

Shown here: Zitron Loft Classic (100% wool; 110 yd [101 m]/50 g): #1223 red (MC), 3 skeins; #1245 light blue, 2 skeins; #1237 light green and #1221 orange, 1 skein each.

NEEDLES
Size U.S. 15 (10 mm). Adjust needle size if necessary to obtain the correct gauge.

NOTIONS
Tapestry needle; needlefelting needle(s); needlefelting foam; cotton pressing cloth; steam iron; ½ yd (.5 m) of coordinating fabric for pillow back; 2½ yd (2.25 m) piping or ½" (1.3 cm) cotton welting; additional 2 yd (2 m) of fabric to cover welting in a continuous strip without seams; quilter's pins; polyester fiberfill; sharp-point sewing needle (or sewing machine) and matching thread.

GAUGE
9½ stitches and 16 rows = 4" (10 cm) in stockinette stitch with two strands of yarn held together, before felting.

Intarsia lets you "paint" colors into your knitting.

PILLOW FRONT

With two strands of MC held tog, CO 48 sts. Purl 1 (WS) row. Work Rows 1–78 of Flora chart. With MC, BO all sts. Weave in all ends securely with tapestry needle to prevent any holes from developing in the felting process.

FINISHING

Felting

Set washing machine for hot-water wash and cold-water rinse at the lowest water level. Add the pillow front along with 1 tablespoon of (nonbleach) detergent and run it through a normal cycle. Remove the piece immediately after the spin cycle so that permanent wrinkles do not develop. Stretch and shape the piece into a perfect rectangle. If necessary, use a hot steam iron to spot-felt less dense areas. Let air-dry completely.

Needlefelting

Place the dry pillow front on top of the needlefelting foam. Following the illustration on page 104, outline each leaf, flower petal, and circle four or five times with the same colors used to knit with as foll: Position about 1" (2.5 cm) of yarn around a motif and punch the felting needle repeatedly through the yarn and the felted pillow front and into the foam pad, felting the yarn to the pillow front as you do so. Cont working around the motif until it is completely outlined, cut the yarn (a little longer than where you intend to stop), and punch the end into the felted pillow front until it disappears within the felted fibers of the front. Add a meandering stem with light green. Add a single strand of red around every flower petal, berry, leaf, circle, and stem. Add randomly placed small dots of orange as shown. When all the needlefelting is complete, cover the pillow with a cotton pressing cloth and use a hot steam iron to set the fibers.

Flora

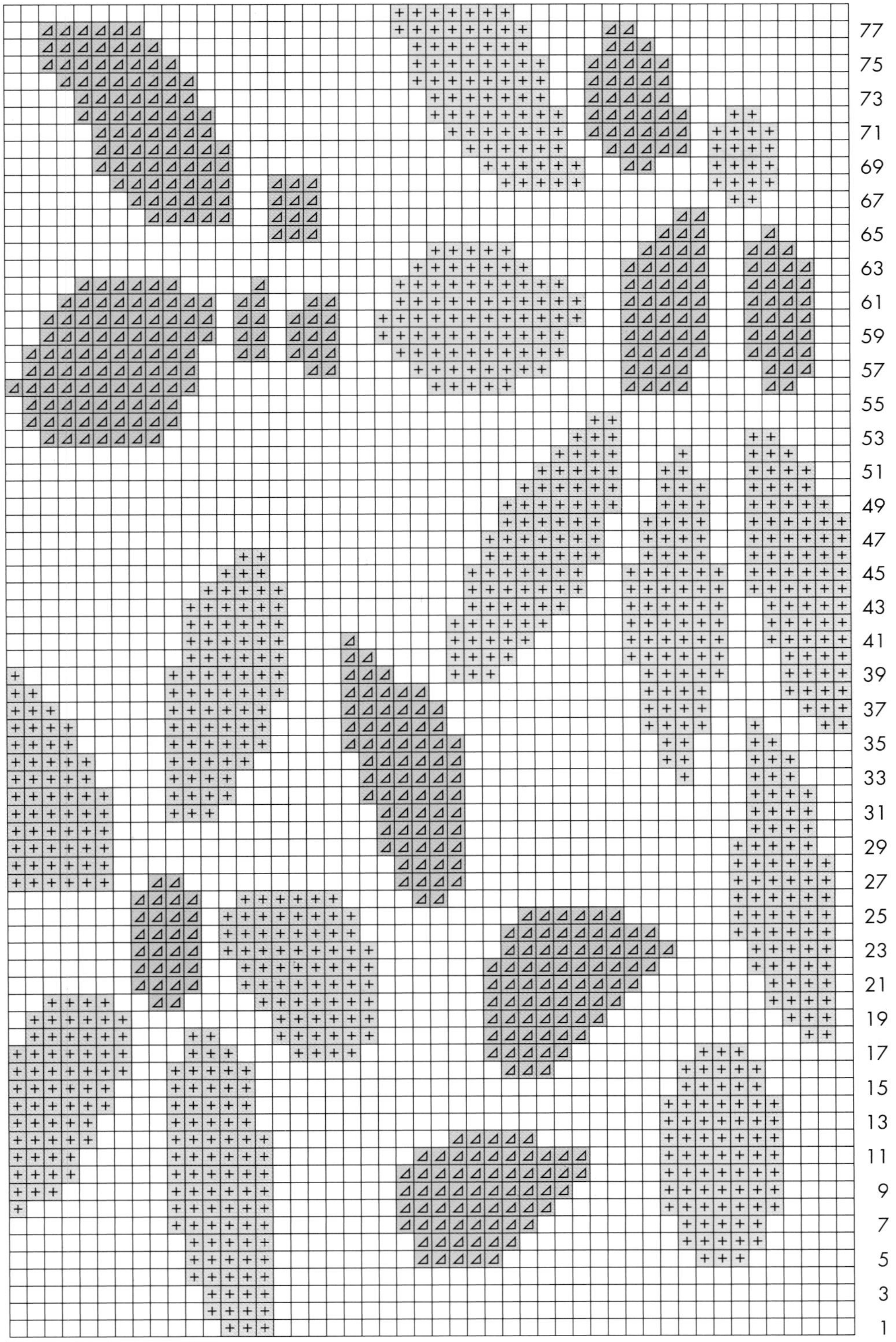

Felting obscures uneven stitches and small gaps between colors in intarsia patterns.

□ MC

+ light blue

△ light green

If you use wool, you can add color and texture with needlefelting.

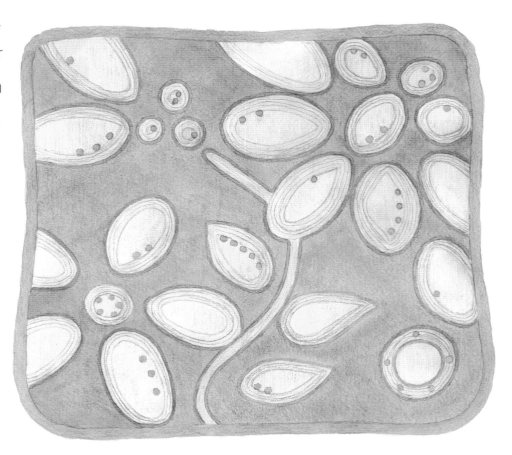

Outline each leaf, petal, and circle with four or five strands of needlefelted yarn. Needlefelt additional spots of orange as desired.

Assembly

Using the pillow front as a guide, cut fabric for pillow back, adding 1" (2.5 cm) to the width and height for seams. Set aside. If using cotton welting, fold the 2 yd (2 m) piece of matching fabric on the bias (corner to corner), iron the fold, and cut a strip 1½" (3.8 cm) from the fold along the entire length. Center the cotton welting along the WS of the bias strip and with sharp-point sewing needle and matching thread, sew as close to the welting as possible to secure it in place. Hand or machine baste the piping or prepared welting to the RS of the pillow front, matching the cut edges of the piping or welting to the edges of the pillow front. With RS tog, pin pillow back to prepared pillow front. Sew the pieces tog as close to the piping or welting as possible, leaving a 6" (15 cm) opening along the bottom edge for stuffing the pillow. Trim excess fabric at corners. Turn pillow RS out and stuff firmly with polyester fiberfill. Sew rem seam as invisibly as possible.

Get color inspiration from nature, textiles, and paintings.

Stripes make for simple knitting, but they become richly impressionistic when worked in variegated yarns. In her simple raglan pullover, **Cecily Glowik** highlighted the subtle colorations of a thick-and-thin self-striping yarn by combining it with a solid color. The sweater is worked in the round from the lower edge to the armholes, then sleeves are added and the yoke is worked in one piece to the neck. The yoke is shaped with paired decreases along raglan lines, a technique that causes the stripes to form distinct "corners" at each set of decreases. The wide ribbed hem is worked on the same number of stitches as the body for a loose, nonbinding fit.

STITCH GUIDE

Stripe Pattern
Rnds 1 and 2: Knit with CC.
Rnds 3 and 4: Knit with MC.
Repeat Rounds 1–4 for pattern.

NOTES

✢ The body is worked in the round from the lower edge to the neck.
✢ When working the stripe pattern, do not cut the yarn at the end of individual stripes; instead let it hang on the wrong side until you are ready to use it again.

BODY

With MC and longer, larger cir needle, CO 128 (144, 160, 176) sts. Place marker (pm) and join for working in rnds, being careful not to twist sts. Rnd begins at side "seam." Work in k4, p4 rib until piece measures 1¾" (4.5 cm). *Next rnd:* K64 (72, 80, 88), pm to denote other side "seam," knit to end. Knit 1 rnd even. Join CC and work in stripe patt (see Stitch Guide) until piece measures 14" (35.5 cm) from CO, ending with Rnd 3 of patt.

FINISHED SIZE
About 30 (34, 37¾, 41½)" (76 [86.5, 96, 105.5] cm) bust circumference. Sweater shown measures 30" (76 cm).

YARN
Worsted weight (#4 Medium).

Shown here: Classic Elite Renaissance (100% wool; 110 yd [101 m]/50 g): #7138 espresso (dark brown; MC), 4 (5, 6, 6) skeins.

Classic Elite Desert (100% wool; 110 yd [101 m]/50 g): #2043 copper canyon (multicolored copper, brown, and sage; CC), 3 (4, 5, 5) balls.

NEEDLES
Body and sleeves—size U.S. 8 (5 mm): 16" and 32" (40 and 80 cm) circular (cir) and set of 4 or 5 double-pointed (dpn). Neckband—size U.S. 7 (4.5 mm): 16" (40 cm) cir. Adjust needle size if necessary to obtain the correct gauge.

NOTIONS
Markers (m); stitch holders; tapestry needle.

GAUGE
17 stitches and 25 rounds = 4" (10 cm) in stockinette-stitch stripe pattern on larger needle, worked in rounds.

To give the appearance of many colors, work stripes with variegated yarn.

Divide for Front and Back

(Rnd 4 of stripe patt) Work to 4 sts before first m, BO next 8 sts (remove m as you come to it), work to 4 sts before next m, BO next 8 sts (remove m as you come to it)—56 (64, 72, 80) sts rem each for front and back. Set aside.

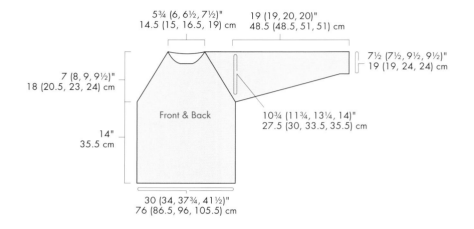

SLEEVES

With MC and dpn, CO 32 (32, 40, 40) sts. Pm and join for working in rnds, being careful not to twist sts. Work in k4, p4 rib until piece measures 1¾" (4.5 cm). Knit 2 rnds even. *Next rnd:* Join CC and work in stripe patt and *at the same time* inc 1 st each side of m on this rnd, then every foll 14 (12, 14, 10)th rnd 6 (8, 7, 9) more times—46 (50, 56, 60) sts. Work even in stripe patt until piece measures 19 (19, 20, 20)" (48.5 [48.5, 51, 51] cm) from CO, ending with Rnd 3 of patt. *Next rnd:* (Rnd 4 of patt) Work to 4 sts before m, BO 8 sts (removing m as you come to it)—38 (42, 48, 52) sts rem. Place sts on holder.

YOKE

With larger cir needle, RS facing, and working according to Rnd 1 of stripe patt, k38 (42, 48, 52) left sleeve sts, pm, k56 (64, 72, 80) front sts, pm, k38 (42, 48, 52) right sleeve sts, pm, k56 (64, 72, 80) back sts—188 (212, 240, 264) sts total. Pm (use a unique color) to denote end of rnd and rejoin for working in rnds. *Dec rnd:* *K2tog, knit to 2 sts before next m, ssk, sl m; rep from * 3 more times—8 sts dec'd. Work 3 rnds even. Rep the last 4 rnds 3 more times—156 (180, 208, 232) sts rem. *Note:* The neck shaping is introduced at the same time as the yoke is shaped; read all the way through the next sections before proceeding. Rep dec rnd every other rnd 12 (15, 18, 20) times, changing to shorter cir needle when necessary and *at the same time*, when piece measures 4 (5, 6, 6½)" (10 [12.5, 15, 16.5] cm) from joining rnd, shape neck as foll.

Shape Neck

Mark center 20 sts of front. *Next rnd:* Cont in patt, work to marked 20 sts, BO these sts, work to end. Working back and forth in rows, cont working yoke decreases every other row, work-ing WS row decs as foll: (WS) Purl to 2 sts before m, p2tog, sl m, ssp (see Glossary, page 135). *At the same time* at each neck edge dec 1 st every RS row 1 (2, 3, 4) time(s)—38 (36, 38, 44) sts rem; 1 (1, 1, 2) st(s) for each front; 6 (4, 4, 4) sts for each sleeve; 24 (26, 28, 32) sts for back. Work even in stripe patt until yoke measures 7 (8, 9, 9½)" (18 [20.5, 23, 24] cm) from joining rnd. BO all sts.

FINISHING

With MC threaded on a tapestry needle, sew underarm seams. Weave in loose ends. Block lightly.

Neckband

With MC, smaller cir needle, and RS facing, pick up and knit 88 (88, 88, 96) sts around neck opening. Pm and join for working in rnds. Work in k4, p4 rib until neckband measures 1" (2.5 cm). BO all sts in patt.

Carry the unused yarn along the wrong side of the work when knitting two-row stripes.

Clusters of sewn-on beads and stem- and chain-stitch embroidery embellish the knitted-in stylized flowers that decorate the backs of **Mags Kandis's** beautiful mittens. Because intarsia motifs are a challenge to work in the round, Mags worked her mittens back and forth and seamed them invisibly along the outside of the hands. She used more stitches for the ribbed cuff than she did for the mittens' hands to create a comfortable, nonbinding fit. Another detail, the contrasting cast-on, adds richness to the design.

NOTE

✛ The color pattern is worked in the intarsia method (see Design Notebook) using different lengths or bobbins of yarn for each color block and twisting the yarns around each other at color changes to prevent holes from forming.

RIGHT MITTEN

With brick red, CO 66 sts.

Cuff

Purl 1 (RS) row, then knit 1 row. Change to MC and knit 1 (RS) row. Cont in rib as foll:
Row 1: (WS) P3, *k4, p4; rep from * to last 7 sts, k4, p3.
Row 2: K3, *p4, k4; rep from * to last 7 sts, p4, k3.
Rep Rows 1 and 2 until piece measures 3" (7.5 cm) from CO, ending with a RS row. Purl 1 (WS) row, dec 2 sts evenly spaced—64 sts rem.

Lower Hand

Using separate lengths (or bobbins) of yarn for each color area, work Rows 1–12 of Right Mitten chart, setting up chart as foll:
Row 1: (RS) K39 according to Row 1 of chart, k25 with MC.
Row 2: P25 with MC, p39 according to Row 2 of chart.
Rows 3–12: Work even as established—piece measures about 4" (10 cm) from CO.

FINISHED SIZE

About 8" (20.5 cm) hand circumference and 10¼" (26 cm) total length. To fit a woman.

YARN

Fingering weight (#1 Super Fine).

Shown here: Brown Sheep Nature Spun Fingering Weight (100% wool; 310 yd [283 m]/50 g): #701 stone (heathered brown; MC), #117 winter blue (medium blue), #101 burnt sienna (brick red), #720 ash (heathered light gray), #104 Grecian olive (dark green), #155 bamboo (pale green), and #N89 roasted coffee (reddish brown), 1 ball each.

NEEDLES

Size U.S. 3 (3.25 mm). Adjust needle size if necessary to obtain the correct gauge.

NOTIONS

Bobbins (optional); stitch holder; markers (m); tapestry needle; sewing needle to apply beads; 61 black opaque size E (6/0) seed beads (available at craft stores).

GAUGE

32 stitches and 44 rows = 4" (10 cm) in stockinette-stitch intarsia pattern.

Thumb Gusset

Cont in patt as established, inc for gusset as foll:

Row 13: K35, place marker (pm), M1 (see Glossary, page 137), k1, M1, pm, knit to end of row—3 gusset sts between markers.

Row 14 and all following WS rows: Purl.

Row 15: K35, slip marker (sl m), M1, k3, M1, sl m, knit to end of row—5 gusset sts between markers.

Row 17: K35, sl m, M1, k5, M1, sl m, knit to end of row—7 gusset sts between markers.

Rows 18–29: Cont to inc 1 st after the first m and 1 st before the second m every RS row in this manner—82 sts after Row 29; 19 gusset sts between markers.

Row 30: Work in patt, removing gusset markers when you come to them.

Row 31: K35, sl next 20 sts onto holder, use the backward-loop method (see Glossary, page 133) to CO 2 sts over gap, knit to end of row—64 sts.

Upper Hand

Rows 32–56: Cont even as established—piece measures about 8" (20.5 cm) from CO.

Shape Top

Cont in patt as established, dec for top as foll:

Row 57: (RS) K1, ssk, k27, k2tog, ssk, k27, k2tog, k1—60 sts rem.

Row 58 and all following WS rows: Purl.

Row 59: K1, ssk, k25, k2tog, ssk, k25, k2tog, k1—56 sts rem.

Row 61: K1, ssk, k23, k2tog, ssk, k23, k2tog, k1—52 sts rem.

Row 63: K1, ssk, k21, k2tog, ssk, k21, k2tog, k1—48 sts rem.

Rows 64–78: Cont to dec 4 sts every RS row in this manner (working 2 fewer sts between decs) until Row 78 of chart has been completed—20 sts rem.

Row 79: *K2tog; rep from * to end of row—10 sts rem.

Cut yarn, leaving an 8" (20.5 cm) tail. Thread tail on a tapestry needle, draw through rem sts, pull tight to close hole, and fasten off on WS.

Thumb

Return 20 held gusset sts to needles. With RS facing, rejoin MC to end of sts, then pick up and knit 2 sts along base of CO sts at top of thumb gap, knit to end—22 sts total. Beg with a WS (purl) row, work even in St st until thumb measures 1¾" (4.5 cm) or ½" (1.3 cm) less than desired total length, ending with a WS row. *Next row:* K1, *k2tog; rep from * to last st, k1—12 sts rem. Purl 1 row. *Next row:* *K2tog; rep from * to end of row—6 sts rem. Cut yarn, leaving an 8" (20.5 cm) tail. Thread tail on a tapestry needle, draw through rem sts, pull tight to close hole, and fasten off on WS.

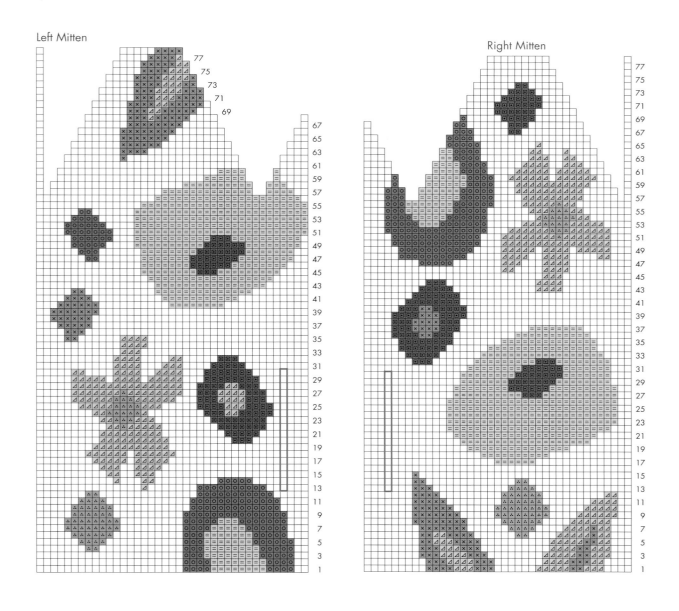

Left Mitten

Right Mitten

| | MC | medium blue | brick red | = heathered light gray | dark green | ◿ pale green | reddish brown | thumb gusset location |

LEFT MITTEN

With brick red, CO 66 sts. Work cuff as for right mitten.

Lower Hand

Using separate lengths (or bobbins) of yarn for each color area, work Rows 1–12 of Left Mitten chart as foll:

Row 1: (RS) K25 with MC, k39 according to Row 1 of chart.

Row 2: P39 according to Row 2 of chart, p25 with MC.

Rows 3–12: Work even as established.

Thumb Gusset

Cont in patt as established, inc for gusset as foll:

Row 13: (RS) K28, pm, M1, k1, M1, pm, knit to end—3 gusset sts between markers.

Row 14 and all following WS rows: Purl.

Row 15: K28, sl m, M1, k3, M1, sl m, knit to end—5 gusset sts between markers.

Row 17: K28, sl m, M1, k5, M1, sl m, knit to end—7 gusset sts between markers.

Rows 18–29: Cont to inc 1 st after the first m and 1 st before the second m every RS row in this manner—82 sts after Row 29; 19 gusset sts between markers.

Row 30: Work in patt, removing gusset markers when you come to them.

Row 31: K28, sl next 20 sts onto holder, use the backward-loop method to CO 2 sts over gap, knit to end—64 sts.

Upper Hand and Thumb

Work as for right mitten.

FINISHING

Weave in loose ends. Block or press lightly.

Embroidery

Work chain stitches and stem stitches (see Glossary, page 135) on motifs as shown in illustration at right.

Beading

Using the same color yarn as the area being worked on, apply beads by stitching them one by one in clusters as shown on illustration and secure.

With MC threaded on a tapestry needle, sew side and thumb seam.

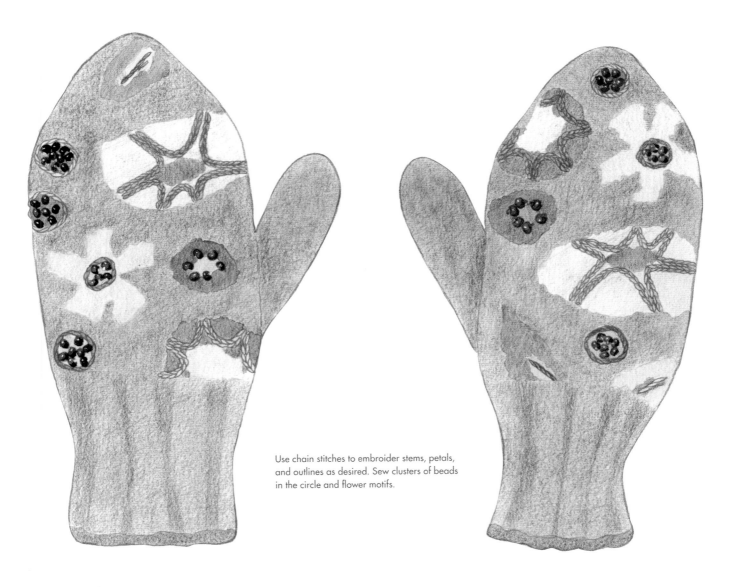

Use chain stitches to embroider stems, petals, and outlines as desired. Sew clusters of beads in the circle and flower motifs.

designNOTEBOOK

GEE'S BEND PULLOVER
mary jane mucklestone

STRIPED RAGLAN
cecily glowik

The varied projects throughout *Color Style* illustrate how different techniques can be used alone or in combination for outstanding results. Even if you're a beginning knitter, there are easy ways to achieve colorful effects. You owe yourself (and your knitting) the benefits of colorwork. If you're unsure about mixing colors, you can draw inspiration from nature, art, textiles, fashion, and interior design.

For starters, try a handpainted or variegated yarn to get the look of complicated colorwork without a lot of fuss. But be aware that the colors in these yarns can pool into blotches or stripes, depending on the length of the color repeats and the number of stitches on your needles. Therefore, many savvy designers combine variegated yarns with solid-colored yarns or in colorwork patterns.

Stripes and slip-stitch patterns require just a bit more concentration than knitting with a single color, but the results are far from simplistic. If you're looking for more of a challenge, try traditional Fair Isle or intarsia techniques. Both require care in maintaining consistent tension, but they offer limitless color possibilities. Finally, add a bit of flair with embroidery or embellishments such as fringe, tassels, or pom-poms. Sometimes just a touch of added color can turn a plain project into a "wow" project.

Stripes are the easiest way to
add color to your knitting.

STRIPES

Stripes are probably the easiest way to add color to your knitting. Except for the additional ends of yarn to weave in, knitting stripes is no different from knitting with a single color. But don't be fooled into thinking that stripes make simple, boring patterns. You can get exciting results by choosing bold bright colors, as in Kristin Nicholas's Hooded Scarf on page 56, by using bands of different widths, as in Mary Jane Mucklestone's Gee's Bend Pullover on page 12, by mixing stripes with other color techniques, as in the yoke and cuffs on Deborah Newton's Honeycomb Turtleneck on page 36 and the shoulder strap of Pam Allen's Funky Fair Isle Bag on page 60, and by working stripes into multicolored ribbing, as in Robin Melanson's Harvest Cardigan on page 46.

To knit stripes, simply change colors at the beginning of a row. You can let a tail of the new color hang loose, or you can secure it to the old color by tying the two together (leaving tails of each to weave in later). Knit with the new color for as many rows as you like, then change to another color. Later, untie any knots, adjust the tension on the edge stitches to match the rest of the row, and weave in the tails. If you weave in the tails along their respective colors, you won't risk the wrong color showing through on the right side of the knitting.

If you're knitting in rows and one color is repeated two or four rows later, you can carry it up the selvedge edge without cutting it, as Cecily Glowik did in her Striped Raglan on page 106. It's not a good idea to carry yarns for more than four rows because the tension of the carried yarn may become too tight or too loose, either of which will distort the edge stitches. If you want to change colors after one or three rows, the yarn will be at the wrong end of the needle, and you'll have to cut it and rejoin it at the beginning of the needle. However, if you're working in rounds where the beginning of the round is adjacent to the end of the round, the yarn will be right where you need it.

STRIPE TIPS

+ If you're working garter stitch, work the color changes on right-side rows so the color change follows a straight line. Otherwise, purl bumps will form a "dotted" line (which you can use as a nice design element, too).

+ An easy way to produce stripes is to make a "magic ball" by tying or splicing together lengths (anywhere from 12 inches to several yards each) of different colors to make a one-of-a-kind multicolored ball of yarn. Knit as usual and watch the colors magically change.

+ Other ways to produce a complicated pattern with stripes include working mitered squares and shadow knitting (see Bibliography, page 142).

+ For a simple twist, change colors somewhere along the middle of the row rather than at the beginning.

Stripes worked in stockinette stitch.

Stripes worked in garter stitch with color changes on right-side rows.

Stripes worked in stockinette and reverse stockinette stitch with color changes on knitted right-side rows.

Stripes worked in stockinette and garter stitch with color changes on right- and wrong-side rows.

HONEYCOMB TURTLENECK
Deborah Newton

SLIP STITCH AND MOSAIC

A simple way to knit stripes that don't look like stripes is to work slip-stitch or mosaic patterns. In this type of color knitting, two contrasting colors—a "dark" color and a "light" color—are alternated every two rows. Following a charted pattern, one of the colors—for example, the dark color—is used to knit certain stitches (e.g., the dark stitches on the chart) and other stitches (e.g., the light stitches) are slipped (transferred from the left needle to the right needle without being knitted). On the next row, the same stitches that were worked on the previous row are worked again (either knitted or purled), and the stitches that were slipped are slipped again. On the next two rows, the other yarn color—for example, the light color—is used, and different stitches (some of which may be the same as the previous two rows) are worked, while others are slipped. Stitches of both colors will appear on your needles even though each row is worked with only one of the colors.

Slip-stitch patterns are appropriate for all types of projects, but because the slipped stitches tend to spread horizontally when blocked, be sure to measure your gauge carefully on a washed and blocked swatch before planning the number of stitches to cast on. Most slip-stitch patterns involve no more than five consecutive slipped stitches to prevent long floats that can cause the fabric to pucker. The slipped stitches tend to appear a little larger than the knitted or purled stitches, which can give slip-stitch patterns a subtle, but often pleasing appearance.

Slip-stitch pattern with both colors worked in stockinette stitch.

Slip-stitch pattern with one color worked in stockinette stitch and the other color worked in garter stitch.

Slip-stitch pattern with both colors worked in garter stitch.

Slip-stitch pattern with one color worked against stripes to give the look of a Fair Isle pattern.

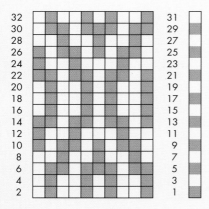

Every row of a slip-stitch chart represents two rows of knitting—a right-side row worked from right to left and a wrong-side row worked from left to right. The vertical bar at the right of the chart indicates which color to use for each two-row sequence.

To begin a slip-stitch pattern, you need to have a foundation row. Typically, this row is worked in one of the colors used for the pattern. The foundation row can be the cast-on row if the stitches aren't already on the needles. The slip-stitch pattern begins with a right-side row and with a different color from the one you used for the foundation row. For example, if you used the light color in the foundation row, you'll use the dark color for the first row of the charted pattern. Follow the first row of the chart, knitting the stitches that are to appear in the working color and slipping the stitches in the original color from the previous row. Always slip the stitches purlwise, and, unless otherwise instructed, always hold the yarn on the wrong side of the work when you slip stitches (Figure 1).

When you get to the end of the row, turn the work around and, for a stockinette-stitch fabric, purl the stitches that were knitted on the previous row and slip the others (Figure 2). The slipped stitches will have been carried for two rows. Change colors on the next row (right side facing), and, following the second row of the chart, knit the stitches of that color and slip the others (Figure 3). Work the return row by purling the worked stitches and slipping the remainder. Because the stitches on the return rows are always worked as they were on the right-side row, slip-stitch charts typically only show the right-side (forward) rows. A column of dark and light squares to the right of slip-stitch charts indicates which color (light or dark) should be used for each two-row sequence.

❖ Slip-stitch patterns show up best if you use two contrasting colors—one light and one dark.

❖ Every row on a slip-stitch chart shows a two-row sequence of knitting; the forward (right-side) row, which is worked from right to left, followed by the return (wrong-side) row, which is worked from left to right.

❖ You can work return rows without looking at the chart—simply work the stitches that were worked on the forward row and slip the stitches that were slipped on the forward row.

❖ When you're slipping stitches, spread out the stitches on the right needle to prevent the floats (the unused yarn) from limiting the elasticity of the fabric.

❖ To keep the selvedges tidy, add an edge stitch to each end of the needle when you work slip-stitch patterns—and knit those edge stitches every row.

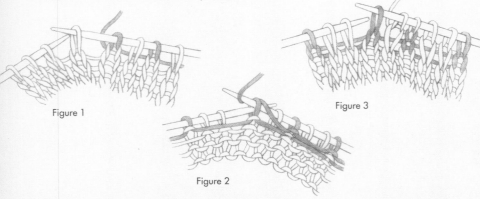

Figure 1

Figure 3

Figure 2

You can add texture to the pattern by knitting (instead of purling) some of the working stitches on wrong-side rows. Véronik Avery worked her slip-stitch patterns on a foundation of garter stitch to give a bumpy texture to her Mosaic Yoke Jacket on page 64. She also worked the yoke in a series of two-color stripes to mimic the look of traditional Fair Isle patterns (see page 124). Jaya Srikrishnan mixed up the knit and purl stitches in her Holi Mitts on page 18. She added visual complexity by working with four colorways of hand-dyed yarns. Deborah Newton worked stockinette bands bordered with garter-stitch ridges to form a honeycomb pattern in the yoke and cuffs of her Honeycomb Turtleneck on page 36.

CUNNINGSBURGH STAR JACKET
Shirley Paden

Fair Isle patterns have double thickness: the yarn in the knitted stitches and the yarn stranded behind the stitches.

FAIR ISLE OR COLOR STRANDING

Traditionally, Fair Isle has been defined as the technique of knitting with many colors but never with more than two colors in any single row. The color that's not in use is carried (or stranded) on the wrong side of the work to make a fabric of double thickness—a layer of knitted stitches on top of a layer of stranded yarns. This type of knitting is named for the particular Shetland Island where the technique is believed to have originated, but the term has come to describe any type of color-stranded knitting, regardless of the number of colors worked in a row.

Traditional Fair Isle patterns quite often showcase large XOX motifs (alternating diagonal and circular patterns) separated by bands of solid colors or smaller "peerie" patterns, as in Mari Lynn Patrick's Mohair Fair Isle on page 22. For a pattern to show up, there must be sufficient contrast between the two colors. For example, in Mary Jane Mucklestone's Retro Andean Pullover on page 88 and Pam Allen's Funky Fair Isle Bag on page 60, a light pattern color shows against a dark background. In Shirley Paden's Cunningsburgh Star Jacket on page 72, a dark pattern color shows against a light background. For a more painterly effect, work the pattern (or background) stitches in a series of colors that shade from dark to light, then to dark again (or vice versa), as in Robin Melanson's Harvest Cardigan on page 46.

Fair Isle technique is also used for small allover patterns such as those Véronik Avery used in her Peace and Love Gloves on page 82. It also is ideal for adding initials, monograms, or phrases. Because there are two layers of yarn throughout—one layer of knitted stitches and one layer of stranded yarn—color stranding is often used to add insulating warmth to mittens, gloves, and hats.

Fair Isle worked with stripes of pattern color against a solid background.

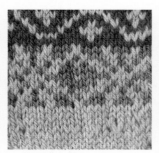

Fair Isle worked with a solid pattern color against stripes of background color.

Fair Isle worked with stripes of pattern color against stripes of background color.

Typically, Fair Isle patterns are worked entirely in stockinette stitch, but the Swedish Bohus designs incorporate purl as well as knit stitches. Chrissy Gardiner used the Bohus technique to add textured relief in the colorful bands in her Bohus-Style Knee-Highs (page 42), and Robin Melanson used purl stitches to punctuate some of the colorwork on her Faux-Embroidery Yoke Sweater (page 30). Véronik Avery took this concept to a new level by working both the pattern and background colors in seed stitch on the body, yoke, and sleeves of her Mosaic Yoke Jacket on page 64.

To knit Fair Isle patterns, alternate between two colors of yarn according to a charted pattern. Work a specified number of stitches with one color, then drop that color. Pick up the other color and work a specified number of stitches, then drop that color and continue with the first color (Figure 1), and so on. This type of knitting is most efficient if you hold and tension both colors of yarn at the same time—either both strands in your right hand (as for the English method of knitting), both strands in your left (as for Continental knitting), or one strand in each hand (Figure 2). Otherwise, you need to re-tension the yarn each time you change colors. If you aren't already familiar with holding two yarns, it's worth taking time to learn before you begin a large project. The time you spend learning to hold two yarns comfortably will be quickly offset by the time you'll save in the long run. A number of books explain the different techniques; see the Bibliography on page 142 for a few.

MOHAIR FAIR ISLE
Mari Lynn Patrick

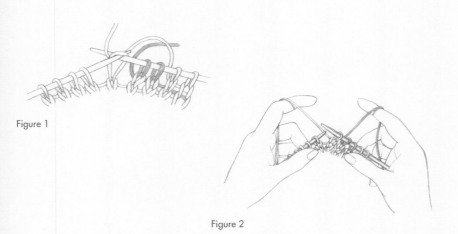

Figure 1

Figure 2

PEACE AND LOVE GLOVES
Véronik Avery

Fair Isle patterns are easiest to work if you tension one yarn in each hand.

FUNKY FAIR ISLE BAG
Pam Allen

Fair Isle patterns typically begin after a single-color foundation row (which can be the cast-on row) worked in the background color. On the first row of pattern, the pattern color is joined to the stitch where it is first used. For example, if the pattern calls for five stitches of the background color followed by three stitches of the pattern color, knit the first five stitches as usual, then join the pattern color (you can simply leave a 6-inch [15-centimeter] tail hanging in the back) and knit the next three stitches. Continue to alternate between the background and pattern colors as specified by the chart. On wrong-side rows, purl instead of knit and carry the floats on the front of the work (along the wrong side of the knitting). When a new color is specified for the background or pattern, simply cut the old color and start with the new, leaving long tails of each hanging down the back of the knitting. Later, when the knitting is complete, weave in the loose ends on the wrong side, preferably along their like colors, being careful to maintain the tension of the knitting so as not to create puckers.

Most small Fair Isle patterns call for color changes at least every 2 inches (5 centimeters). However, some large patterns call for one color to strand longer distances, which can result in long floats on the wrong side that can catch and pull on fingers, buttons, or jewelry and cause the design to pucker on the right side. To prevent long floats, it's a good idea to catch the two yarns together every five stitches or so to hold the float close to the fabric, especially if you're working with slippery yarns. If you use the Continental method of tensioning at least one of the yarns in your left hand as you knit, you can catch the yarns as you knit by lifting the stranded color above the right needle as you knit with the working color (Figure 1), then lowering the strand and knitting the next stitch (Figure 2) so that the stranded yarn is caught between the two stitches. Do not catch the floats between the same two stitches on subsequent rows or you may produce an unintended vertical "line."

Figure 1

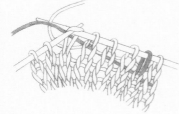

Figure 2

FAUX-EMBROIDERY YOKE SWEATER
Robin Melanson

The key to successful Fair Isle knitting is maintaining constant tension—not only between the pattern and background yarns, but also between right-side and wrong-side rows. The constant tension required means that you need to purl and carry floats along the wrong side of the work at the same tension that you knit and carry floats along the right side of the work. Most tension problems arise from not carrying the unused yarn loosely enough across the back of the work. The pattern stitches then pucker above the background stitches instead of lying along the same plane and the fabric can pull in widthwise. The easiest way to combat these tension problems is to stretch the stitches as far as possible on the right needle at each color change to ensure that the stranded color spans the same width as the knitted stitches.

Most knitters agree that it's easier to strand colors on right-side than on wrong-side rows. When you add the complication that many knitters knit a bit more tightly than they purl (or vice versa), it's easy to see why many Fair Isle projects are worked in the round. That way, the right side is always facing the knitter and all stitches are knitted. For projects that involve shaping (i.e., necklines or armholes) or for cardigans such as Robin Melanson's Harvest Cardigan on page 46, steeks are added to the regular stitches. Steeks are extra stitches (usually between five and nine stitches) that provide a space for the knitting to be cut open without interrupting the patterning or forfeiting inches in circumference; see the sidebar on page 126 for details. The steek stitches then become facings along the cut edges.

FAIR ISLE TIPS

❖ Avoid extremely high-contrast yarns (e.g., black and white) in which the floats (especially long floats in which the colors are caught around each other) might show through to the right side.

❖ Use variegated yarns to give the impression of more colors.

❖ To make the pattern prominent (and to prevent unnecessary tangles), always pick up the pattern color from below the background color and always pick up the background color from above the pattern color.

❖ To manage two balls of yarn, place one on each side of you, or place one on the chair next to you and the other on the floor, or place each ball in a separate box or container so the balls don't bounce around and tangle with each other.

❖ Most knitters get a slightly tighter gauge when they work Fair Isle patterns than they do when they work stockinette stitch. If you plan to combine bands of Fair Isle and stockinette stitch, check your gauge on both stitch patterns. You may need to use larger needles or more stitches for the Fair Isle sections.

❖ To ensure that the stranded yarn spans the same distance as the knitted stitches, stretch the stitches on your right needle when you change colors.

❖ To ensure that colors don't run (which happens particularly with reds, blues, and blacks), test the colorfastness of the yarn before beginning. Simply wet a piece of yarn with warm water and blot it with a clean paper towel. If any color runs onto the towel, you may want to choose a different yarn, especially if you want to pair any of these colors with bleached white.

❖ To tame tangled yarns, hold the two balls up in the air and let the knitting spin around until the tangles disappear.

❖ Weave in the ends as you go so you won't have so many tails to weave in later.

HARVEST CARDIGAN
Robin Melanson

By using steeks, you can knit cardigans in the round.

WORKING STEEKS

Most books on Fair Isle knitting include instructions for working steeks; see the Bibliography on page 143 for a few.

In general, to work a steek, add five to nine stitches (more for slippery yarn such as alpaca; fewer for sticky yarns such as wool) to the number of stitches to be cast on. For a wool cardigan, for example, cast on seven more stitches than specified by the pattern. Work the pattern in rounds, alternating one stitch of each color used in each row in a striped or checkerboard pattern across the seven steek stitches (Figure 1). Doing so maintains even tension on both colors throughout these extra stitches.

Work the pattern to the armholes as specified. If the pattern has drop-shoulder shaping, simply add seven more steek stitches along each side "seam." If the pattern calls for a number of stitches to be bound off at each armhole, go ahead and bind off those stitches, then cast on seven more steek stitches on the next round. You will now have twenty-one extra stitches, seven each in three steeks—one steek at the center front and one steek at each armhole (Figure 2). Work the new steek stitches by alternating one stitch of each color as for the center front steek. Continue working the pattern as specified (working decreases each side of the armhole steeks, if necessary) to the beginning of the neck shaping. If the pattern calls for a number of stitches to be bound off at the center front neck, bind off those stitches along with the original seven steek stitches, then cast on seven more steek stitches on the next round. To shape the neck, continue working in rounds, working decreases as specified on each side of the steek stitches (Figure 3). Continue to work in rounds to the top of the shoulders.

Before you cut along the steek stitches, you'll want to reinforce them to ensure that they don't ravel, especially if you used a slippery yarn such as alpaca, cotton, or a synthetic. You can reinforce steek stitches a number of ways; one of the easiest is to baste along the center of the steek with a smooth contrasting yarn (Figure 4). If your steek has an odd number of stitches, you'll baste along the center stitch of the steek; if your steek has an even number of stitches, you'll baste between the center two stitches. Using a sewing machine set for straight stitches, machine-stitch one stitch away from the basting yarn to secure the knitting (Figure 5). With sharp scissors, carefully cut along the basting yarn at the center of the steek, cutting a few rows of knitting at a time and being careful not to cut through the machine stitches (Figure 6). Turn the extra steek stitches to the inside of the knitting and baste in place (Figure 7). Voilà! You're ready to add the sleeves, neckband, and buttonband.

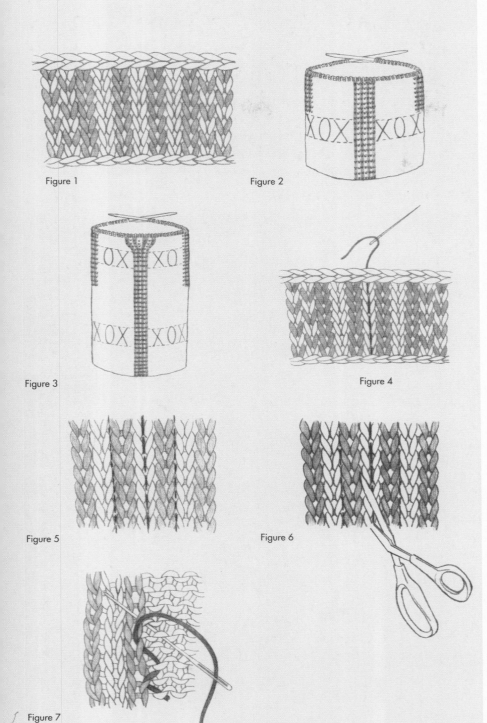

Figure 1

Figure 2

Figure 3

Figure 4

Figure 5

Figure 6

Figure 7

Steeks are extra stitches that provide space for the knitting to be cut open without interrupting the pattern or forfeiting inches in circumference.

RETRO ANDEAN PULLOVER
Mary Jane Mucklestone

ARGYLE VEST
Ann Budd

INTARSIA

The intarsia method of knitting is used to create isolated areas of colors. Unlike Fair Isle knitting, the yarns are not stranded across the back of the work. Instead, you work each color block with a separate ball or bobbin of yarn. Each color is worked for the desired number of stitches, then dropped, and the next color is picked up and worked for the desired number of stitches, then dropped, and so on. (To prevent holes from forming at the color changes, twist the two yarns around one another to lock the adjacent stitches together.) Although there's no limit to the number of colors you can work in a single row, there may be a limit to the number of balls of yarn you want to manage.

The intarsia technique is used to create vertical stripes, pictorial designs (as in Mary Jane Mucklestone's Retro Andean Pulllover on page 88), and argyle patterns, as in Ann Budd's Argyle Vest on page 94.

To knit an intarsia pattern, you'll need a separate ball of yarn for each block of color. To minimize tangles, most knitters work with partial balls wound onto bobbins or into butterflies (see box on page 130) instead of full balls of yarn. The first row of an intarsia pattern is typically worked on a right-side row. Work the first color for the desired number of stitches, let that bobbin or butterfly of yarn drop to the back of the work, pick up a new bobbin or butterfly for the second color (leave a tail hanging in the back to work in later) and work that color for the desired number of stitches, then let that one drop to the back. Pick up a new bobbin or butterfly for the third color (even if it's the same color as the first block of stitches) from underneath the previous color and work that one for the desired number of stitches, then let that yarn drop to the back—and so on to the end of the row (Figure 1).

If you look at the row just knitted, you'll see that all of the bobbins or butterflies are attached to the left (ending) edge of their respective color blocks. The tails from the beginning of these yarns will be hanging from the right, or beginning, edge of the blocks. When you turn the work around to work the next (wrong-side) row, the bobbins or butterflies will be at the beginning edge of each block, right where you'll need them to continue knitting. To work the next row, follow the next row of the charted pattern and purl to the first color change, drop the yarn just used and pick up the next color from beneath the one just dropped (Figure 2)

Figure 1

Figure 2

so the yarns twist and hide potential gaps at color changes. Purl the desired number of stitches with the second color, then change to the next color, again picking up the new yarn from under the one just used.

For simplicity, many intarsia patterns are designed so that wrong-side rows duplicate the color placement of the previous right-side rows so you don't need to refer to the chart for the return row. Simply work the first set of stitches with the same yarn that ended the previous row, drop that yarn and pick up the next color from under that strand so that the yarns twist around each other close to the needles, work the next set of stitches with the new ball, twist the yarns at the next color change, and so on to the end of the row. For the first few rows, be careful to always pick up the strand of yarn that's connected to the bobbin or butterfly, not the tail end (otherwise, you'll run out of working yarn).

After you've knitted a couple of rows, you'll see why intarsia is typically worked back and forth in rows. If you were to work it in rounds (where the right side of the work is always facing you), the working yarn would be attached to the far side of each color block at the end of the round, not at the beginning of each block—where it will be needed for the next round. There are advanced techniques that let you work intarsia in rounds (see the Bibliography on page 142), but they're beyond the scope of this book.

The key to successful intarsia colorwork is to maintain constant tension at color changes. Because each block of color is worked with its own "ball" of yarn, the stitches at the edges of each block are similar to edge stitches in single-color knitting. The difference is that these edge stitches occur in the middle of the row, not at the sides where they would be hidden in seams. For most knitters, edge stitches are typically a little looser or a little tighter than stitches in the center of a row. Therefore, it's important to carefully tension the stitches at the color changes to match the tension in the center of the color blocks. In general, tension problems are less noticeable when the color changes occur along diagonal lines (where edge stitches are offset from one another) than when they follow vertical lines (where edge stitches are stacked on top of one another).

❖ Before you begin knitting, identify the areas of the chart that require separate colors and prepare the yarn for each section in advance so you can work uninterrupted to the end of the row.

❖ Instead of using full balls of yarn that tangle more quickly and more severely, wind yarn onto bobbins or butterflies (see page 130).

❖ For small areas of color, use loose 2- to 3-foot (60- to 90-centimeter) lengths of yarn that are easy to pull out of tangles.

❖ For very small areas of pattern, consider adding the color with duplicate stitch after the knitting is completed.

❖ Before beginning each row, familiarize yourself with the chart to identify areas where the color blocks shift to the left and areas where they shift to the right so you don't knit past a color change.

❖ To help untangle yarns, hold the knitting in one hand over your head and use the other hand to "comb" apart separate strands, butterflies, or bobbins.

❖ Weave in loose ends along similar colors on the wrong side of the knitting.

❖ If you work with cotton or other slippery yarns, leave a tail at least ½ inch (1.3 centimeters) long hanging on the wrong side after weaving in the loose ends. A shorter end might work through to the right side as the garment is worn.

Intarsia worked as color blocks.

Intarsia worked as diagonal stripes.

Intarsia worked pictorially.

HOW TO WIND BOBBINS AND BUTTERFLIES

Bobbin

Use a commercial bobbin or make your own by cutting out a rectangle of cardboard and cutting notches in each short end. Wrap the yarn around the bobbin, guiding it between the slits in each notched end. To use the bobbin, unwind enough yarn to knit the number of stitches in the color block, then secure the end in the slit.

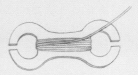

Butterfly

Place a tail of yarn in the palm of one hand with the end near your wrist and hold it with your last three fingers while holding your thumb and index finger out straight. With the other hand, wrap the yarn around your thumb and index finger in a figure-eight pattern until the butterfly is the desired size (Figure 1). Remove the butterfly and hold it in the middle while you wrap the end firmly around the center. Cut the yarn, leaving a short tail. Twist the tail into a loop and wrap the yarn around the bundle in the opposite direction (Figure 2), slip the end through the loop (Figure 3), and pull tight to secure. You can pull the yarn easily from the center of the butterfly, beginning with the end that was in the palm of your hand.

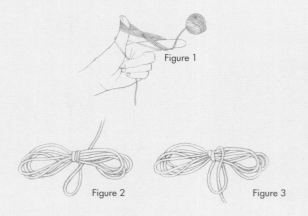

Figure 1

Figure 2

Figure 3

EMBELLISHMENTS

You can add all sorts of color with embroidery, fringe, tassels, or pom-poms after you knit. Such embellishments can spruce up an otherwise plain garment. Kristin Nicholas added another layer of color to her Hooded Scarf on page 56 by embroidering vines and flowers on top of the Fair Isle pattern. Véronik Avery took a more subtle approach and embroidered a single flower on one of her Peace and Love Gloves (page 82).

Needlefelting is an alternative to embroidery on felted knitting. Marta McCall needlefelted borders around each of the intarsia motifs on the Floral Pillow (page 100) to smooth out the edges of the color changes. She also used needlefelting to add dots of bright color to the petals.

Don't overlook adding color the easy way with fringe, tassels, and pom-poms. Use the same colors you used for the body of the project or introduce new ones that coordinate

HOODED SCARF
Kristin Nicholas

or contrast. Kristin Nicholas worked knotted fringe at the ends of her Hooded Scarf (page 56) and topped it off with a multicolored tassel. Shirley Paden sewed colorful pom-poms to the ends of the I-cord belt in her Cunningsburgh Star Jacket (page 72).

FINISHING

When you've finished knitting, weave in the loose ends of yarn by working them in on the wrong side along like colors, making sure that the colors don't show through to the right side and being careful not to pull the ends so tight as to cause puckers. After weaving in a few ends, turn the work over to check that the stitches lie flat and that the woven-in ends aren't visible on the right side. Trim the ends, leaving about ½ inch (1.3 centimeters) hanging to ensure that the ends don't work their way to the right side when the piece is blocked.

No matter which type of color work you've used, you'll want to block the knitting to "set" the yarns. Let the knitted piece soak in lukewarm water for twenty minutes or longer to ensure that the yarn is thoroughly wet. Squeeze out the water, then roll the piece in a bath towel to remove excess moisture. Lay the piece flat and let it air-dry thoroughly. When dry, trim the loose ends close to the knitting if desired.

Add even more color with fringe, tassels, pom-poms, embroidery, and needlefelting.

FUN FLOWER MITTENS
Mags Kandis

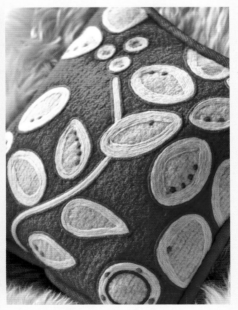

FLORAL PILLOW
Marta McCall

ABBREVIATIONS

beg(s)	begin(s); beginning		rem	remain(s); remaining
BO	bind off		rep	repeat(s); repeating
CC	contrasting color		rev St st	reverse stockinette stitch
cm	centimeter(s)		rnd(s)	round(s)
cn	cable needle		RS	right side
CO	cast on		sl	slip
cont	continue(s); continuing		sl st	slip st (slip 1 stitch purlwise unless otherwise indicated)
dec(s)	decrease(s); decreasing		ssk	slip 2 stitches knitwise, one at a time, from the left needle to right needle, insert left needle tip through both front loops and knit together from this position (1 stitch decrease)
dpn	double-pointed needles			
foll	follow(s); following			
g	gram(s)		st(s)	stitch(es)
inc(s)	increase(s); increasing		St st	stockinette stitch
k	knit		tbl	through back loop
k1f&b	knit into the front and back of same stitch		tog	together
kwise	knitwise, as if to knit		WS	wrong side
m	marker(s)		wyb	with yarn in back
MC	main color		wyf	with yarn in front
mm	millimeter(s)		yd	yard(s)
M1	make one (increase)		yo	yarnover
p	purl		*	repeat starting point
p1f&b	purl into front and back of same stitch		* *	repeat all instructions between asterisks
patt(s)	pattern(s)		( )	alternate measurements and/or instructions
psso	pass slipped stitch over		[ ]	work instructions as a group a specified number of times
pwise	purlwise, as if to purl			

BIND-OFFS

Three-Needle Bind-Off

Place the stitches to be joined onto two separate needles and hold the needles parallel so that the right sides of knitting face together. Insert a third needle into the first stitch on each of two needles **(Figure 1)** and knit them together as one stitch **(Figure 2)**, *knit the next stitch on each needle the same way, then use the left needle tip to lift the first stitch over the second and off the needle **(Figure 3)**. Repeat from * until no stitches remain on first two needles. Cut yarn and pull tail through last stitch to secure.

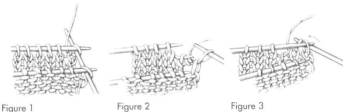

Figure 1   Figure 2   Figure 3

CAST-ONS

Backward-Loop Cast-On

*Loop working yarn and place it on needle backward so that it doesn't unwind. Repeat from *.

Cable Cast-On

Hold needle with working yarn in your left hand with the wrong side of the work facing you. *Insert right needle between the first two stitches on left needle **(Figure 1)**, wrap yarn around needle as if to knit, draw yarn through **(Figure 2)**, and place new loop on left needle **(Figure 3)** to form a new stitch. Repeat from * for the desired number of stitches, always working between the first two stitches on the left needle.

Figure 1   Figure 2   Figure 3

Invisible Provisional Cast-On

Make a loose slipknot of working yarn and place it on the right needle. Hold a length of contrasting waste yarn next to the slipknot and around your left thumb; hold working yarn over your left index finger. *Bring the right needle forward, then under waste yarn, over working yarn, grab a loop of working yarn and bring it forward under working yarn **(Figure 1)**, then bring needle back behind the working yarn and grab a second loop **(Figure 2)**. Repeat from * for the desired number of stitches. When you're ready to work in the opposite direction, place the exposed loops on a knitting needle as you pull out the waste yarn.

Figure 1   Figure 2

DECREASES

Knit 2 Together (k2tog)

Knit two stitches together as if they were a single stitch.

Slip, Slip, Knit (ssk)

Slip two stitches individually knitwise (**Figure 1**), insert left needle tip into the front of these two slipped stitches, and use the right needle to knit them together through their back loops (**Figure 2**).

Figure 1   Figure 2

Slip, Slip, Slip, Knit (sssk)

Slip three stitches individually knitwise (**Figure 1**), insert left needle tip into the front of these three slipped stitches, and use the right needle to knit them together through their back loops (**Figure 2**).

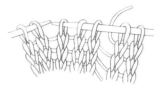 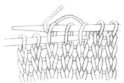

Figure 1   Figure 2

Slip, Slip, Purl (ssp)

Holding yarn in front, slip two stitches individually knitwise (**Figure 1**), then slip these two stitches back onto left needle (they will be turned on the needle) and purl them together through their back loops (**Figure 2**).

Figure 1   Figure 2

EMBROIDERY

Backstitch

Bring threaded needle out from back to front between the first two knitted stitches you want to cover. *Insert the needle at the right edge of the right stitch to be covered, then bring it back out at the left edge of the second stitch. Insert the needle again between these two stitches and bring it out between the next two to be covered. Repeat from *.

Blanket Stitch

Working from left to right, bring threaded needle in and out of the knitted background, always keeping the needle on top of the yarn.

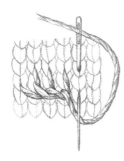

Chain Stitch

Bring threaded needle out from back to front at center of a knitted stitch. Form a short loop and insert needle back where it came out. Keeping the loop under the needle, bring needle back out in center of next stitch to the right.

French Knot

Bring threaded needle out of knitted background from back to front, wrap yarn around needle one to three times, and use your thumb to hold the wraps in place while you insert needle into background a short distance from where it came out. Pull the needle through the wraps into the background.

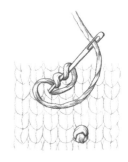

Daisy Stitch

*Bring threaded needle out of knitted background from back to front, form a short loop and insert needle into background where it came out. Keeping the loop under the needle, bring the needle back out of the background a short distance away (**Figure 1**), pull loop snug, and insert needle into fabric on far side of loop. Beginning each stitch at the same point in the background, repeat from * for the desired number of petals (**Figure 2**; six petals shown).

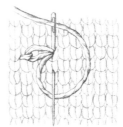

Figure 1

Figure 2

Stem Stitch

Bring threaded needle out of knitted background from back to front at the center of a knitted stitch. *Insert the needle into the upper right edge of the next stitch to the right, then out again at the center of the stitch below. Repeat from * as desired.

Straight Stitch

*Bring threaded needle out of knitted background from back to front at the base of the stitches to be covered, then in from front to back at the tip of the stitches to be covered. Repeat from *, working in straight lines or radiating from a point as desired.

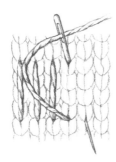

Woven Web

Work five equal-length straight stitches radiating out from the same point on the knitted background to form a star, then weave the threaded needle over and under the straight stitches to fill in the center of the initial star.

Figure 1   Figure 2

GRAFTING

Kitchener Stitch

Arrange stitches on two needles so that there is the same number of stitches on each needle. Hold the needles parallel to each other with wrong sides of the knitting together. Allowing about ½" (1.3 cm) per stitch to be grafted, thread matching yarn on a tapestry needle. Work from right to left as follows:

Step 1:. Bring tapestry needle through the first stitch on the front needle as if to purl and leave the stitch on the needle (Figure 1).

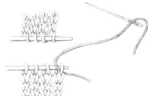

Figure 1

Step 2: Bring tapestry needle through the first stitch on the back needle as if to knit and leave that stitch on the needle (Figure 2).

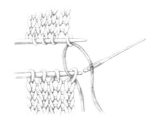

Step 3: Bring tapestry needle through the first front stitch as if to knit and slip this stitch off the needle, then bring tapestry needle through the next front stitch as if to purl and leave this stitch on the needle (Figure 3).

Figure 2

Step 4: Bring tapestry needle through the first back stitch as if to purl and slip this stitch off the needle, then bring tapestry needle through the next back stitch as if to knit and leave this stitch on the needle (Figure 4).

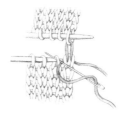

Figure 3

Repeat Steps 3 and 4 until one stitch remains on each needle, adjusting the tension to match the rest of the knitting as you go. To finish, bring tapestry needle through the front stitch as if to knit and slip this stitch off the needle, then bring tapestry needle through the back stitch as if to purl and slip this stitch off the needle.

Figure 4

INCREASES

Raised Make-One—Left Slant (M1L)

Note: Use the left slant if no direction of slant is specified.

With left needle tip, lift the strand between the last knitted stitch and the first stitch on the left needle from front to back (**Figure 1**), then knit the lifted loop through the back (**Figure 2**).

Figure 1

Figure 2

Raised Make-One—Right Slant (M1R)

With left needle tip, lift the strand between the needles from back to front (**Figure 1**). Knit the lifted loop through the front (**Figure 2**).

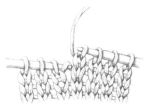

Figure 1

Figure 2

Raised Make-One Purlwise (M1 pwise)

With left needle tip, lift the strand between the needles from front to back (**Figure 1**), then purl the lifted loop through the back (**Figure 2**).

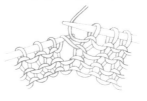

Figure 1

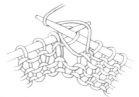

Figure 2

NO STITCH

Many charted stitch patterns involve increases or decreases that cause the stitch count, and consequently the number of boxes in a chart, to vary from one row to the next. When adding or subtracting boxes at the edge of a chart disrupts the vertical alignment of symbols in the chart, "no stitch" symbols may be used. "No stitch" symbols are placed within the borders of a chart so that stitches that are aligned vertically in the knitting will appear aligned vertically in the chart. The no stitch symbol accommodates a "missing" stitch while maintaining the vertical integrity of the pattern. In this book, missing stitches are represented by gray shaded boxes. When you come to a shaded box in a chart, simply skip over it and continue to the end of the row as if it doesn't exist.

PICK UP AND KNIT

Pick Up and Knit Along CO or BO Edge

With right side facing and working from right to left, insert the tip of the needle into the center of the stitch below the bind-off or cast-on edge (**Figure 1**), wrap yarn around needle, and pull through a loop (**Figure 2**). Pick up one stitch for every existing stitch.

Figure 1

Figure 2

Pick Up and Knit Along Shaped Edge

With right side facing and working from right to left, insert tip of needle between last and second-to-last stitches, wrap yarn around needle, and pull through a loop. Pick up and knit about three stitches for every four rows, adjusting as necessary so that picked-up edge lays flat.

PICK UP AND PURL

With wrong side of work facing and working from right to left, *insert needle tip under selvedge stitch from the far side to the near side, wrap yarn around needle (**Figure 1**), and pull a loop through (**Figure 2**). Repeat from * for desired number of stitches.

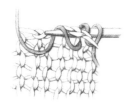

Figure 1

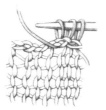

Figure 2

POM-POM

Cut two circles of cardboard, each ½" (1.3 cm) larger than desired finished pom-pom width. Cut a small circle out of the center and a small wedge out of the side of each circle (**Figure 1**). Tie a strand of yarn between the circles, hold circles together and wrap with yarn— the more wraps, the thicker the pom-pom. Cut between the circles and knot the tie strand tightly (**Figure 2**). Place pom-pom between two smaller cardboard circles held together with a needle and trim the edges (**Figure 3**). This technique comes from *Nicky Epstein's Knitted Embellishments*, Interweave, 1999.

Figure 1

Figure 2

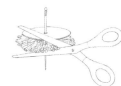

Figure 3

SEAMS

Mattress Stitch

Place the pieces to be seamed on a table, right sides facing up. Begin at the lower edge and work upward as follows for your stitch pattern:

Stockinette Stitch with 1-Stitch Seam Allowance

Insert threaded needle under one bar between the two edge stitches on one piece, then under the corresponding bar plus the bar above it on the other piece (**Figure 1**). *Pick up the next two bars on the first piece (**Figure 2**), then the next two bars on the other (**Figure 3**). Repeat from *, ending by picking up the last bar or pair of bars on the first piece.

Figure 1

Figure 2

Figure 3

Stockinette Stitch with ½-Stitch Seam Allowance

To reduce bulk in the mattress-stitch seam, work as for the 1-stitch seam allowance but pick up the bars in the center of the edge stitches instead of between the last two stitches.

Whipstitch

Hold pieces to be sewn together so that the edges to be seamed are even with each other. With yarn threaded on a tapestry needle, *insert needle through both layers from back to front, then bring needle to back. Repeat from *, keeping even tension on the seaming yarn.

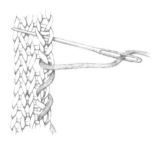

SHORT-ROWS

Knit Side

Work to turning point, slip next stitch purlwise (**Figure 1**), bring the yarn to the front, then slip the same stitch back to the left needle (**Figure 2**), turn the work around and bring the yarn in position for the next stitch—one stitch has been wrapped and the yarn is correctly positioned to work the next stitch. When you come to a wrapped stitch on a subsequent row, hide the wrap by working it together with the wrapped stitch as follows: Insert right needle tip under the wrap (from the front if wrapped stitch is a knit stitch; from the back if wrapped stitch is a purl stitch; **Figure 3**), then into the stitch on the needle, and work the stitch and its wrap together as a single stitch.

Figure 1

Figure 2

Figure 3

Purl Side

Work to the turning point, slip the next stitch purlwise to the right needle, bring the yarn to the back of the work (**Figure 1**), return the slipped stitch to the left needle, bring the yarn to the front between the needles (**Figure 2**), and turn the work so that the knit side is facing—one stitch has been wrapped and the yarn is correctly positioned to knit the next stitch. To hide the wrap on a subsequent purl row, work to the wrapped stitch, use the tip of the right needle to pick up the wrap from the back, place it on the left needle (**Figure 3**), then purl it together with the wrapped stitch.

Figure 1

Figure 2

Figure 3

TASSEL

Cut a piece of cardboard 4" (10 cm) wide by the desired length of the tassel plus 1" (2.5 cm). Wrap yarn to desired thickness around cardboard. Cut a short length of yarn and tie tightly around one end of wrapped yarn (**Figure 1**). Cut yarn loops at other end. Cut another piece of yarn and wrap tightly around loops a short distance below top knot to form tassel neck. Knot securely, thread ends onto tapestry needle, and pull to center of tassel (**Figure 2**). Trim ends.

Figure 1

Figure 2

CONTRIBUTING DESIGNERS

Pam Allen is the creative director for Classic Elite Yarns and the former editor in chief of *Interweave Knits*. She's the author of *Knitting for Dummies* and *Scarf Style*, and coauthor of *Wrap Style*, *Lace Style*, and *Bag Style*.

Véronik Avery has been designing knitwear for just five years. She is the former creative director for JCA Yarns and author of *Knitting Classic Style*. Véronik lives in Montréal, Québec.

Ann Budd is a book editor for Interweave. She is the author of *The Knitter's Handy Book* series and *Getting Started Knitting Socks*, and coauthor of *Wrap Style*, *Lace Style*, and *Bag Style*. Ann lives in Boulder, Colorado.

Chrissy Gardiner designs knitwear and tries to keep up with her two small children in Portland, Oregon. You can find more of her work at gardineryarnworks.com.

Cecily Glowik has a BFA in painting, but knitting is her passion. She has been designing handknits for more than ten years and has had numerous designs featured in books, magazines, and Classic Elite Yarns collections.

Mags Kandis is the head designer and consultant for Mission Falls Yarns. She is the author of numerous knitting books, including *Folk Style*. Mags lives in Ontario, Canada.

Marta McCall is passionate about the process of invention—including merging varied craft techniques with knitting. She designs for knitting magazines and yarn companies and publishes her modern and innovative knitwear patterns through her online company, TinkkniT.com.

Robin Melanson is the author of *Knitting New Mittens and Gloves*. She lives and works in Toronto, Ontario. Visit her website at robinmelanson.com.

Mary Jane Mucklestone is a photographer's assistant and stylist and an avid knitter. Get to know her at Mary Jane, Midge & Mink (maryjane midgemink.blogspot.com).

Deborah Newton, author of *Designing Knitwear*, has been a professional knitwear designer since 1980. She lives in Providence, Rhode Island.

Kristin Nicholas is a knitwear and stitchery author and designer. She lives in western Massachusetts with her husband and daughter, along with sheep, pigs, chickens, border collies, and farm cats. Visit her website at kristinnicholas.com.

Shirley Paden is the owner of Shirley Paden Custom Knits in New York City. She teaches master knitting classes for the fashion industry and conducts seminars on lace, entrelac, cables, color knitting, and finishing.

Mari Lynn Patrick studied knitwear design at a guild school in Leicester, England, in the early 1970s. Since then she has designed for magazines and yarn companies. Mari Lynn lives in Baltimore, Maryland.

Jaya Srikrishnan is an accomplished designer and teacher who loves to share her expertise and enthusiasm with other knitters. Her designs have been published in several magazines and books.

BROWN SHEEP COMPANY
100662 County Rd. 16
Mitchell, NE 69357
brownsheep.com

CLASSIC ELITE YARNS
122 Western Ave.
Lowell, MA 01851
classiceliteyarns.com

DIAMOND YARN
9697 St. Laurent, Ste. 101
Montréal, QC
Canada H3L 2N1
and
155 Martin Ross, Unit 3
Toronto, ON
Canada M3J 2L9
diamondyarn.com

JCA INC./REYNOLDS
35 Scales Ln.
Townsend, MA 01469
jcacrafts.com

LORNA'S LACES
4229 North Honore St.
Chicago, IL 60613
lornaslaces.net

SIMPLY SHETLAND
18435 Olympic Ave. South
Seattle, WA 98188
simplyshetland.net

SKACEL COLLECTION
PO Box 88110
Seattle, WA 98138
skacelknitting.com

**WESTMINSTER FIBERS/
NASHUA/ROWAN**
165 Ledge St.
Nashua, NH 03060
westminsterfibers.com
In Canada: Diamond Yarn

BIBLIOGRAPHY

Allen, Pam. *Knitting for Dummies.* New York: Wiley, 2002.
—Excellent introduction to all types of knitting.

Bartlett, Roxana. *Slip-Stitch Knitting.* Loveland, Colorado: Interweave, 1998.
—A solid foundation for working slip-stitch patterns and designing your own.

Compton, Rae. *The Complete Book of Traditional Knitting.* New York: Charles Scribner's Sons, 1983.
—A general overview of a number of traditional techniques, including color stranding (Fair Isle).

Epstein, Nicky. *Nicky Epstein's Knitted Embellishments: 350 Appliqués, Borders, Cords and More!* Loveland, Colorado: Interweave, 1999.
—Includes all sorts of embellishments, including detailed illustrations for working embroidery on knitted fabrics.

Feitelson, Ann. *The Art of Fair Isle Knitting.* Loveland, Colorado: Interweave, 1996.
—Everything you need to know about Fair Isle knitting plus eighteen original patterns.

Gibson-Roberts, Priscilla. "Traditional Techniques for Creating Ethnic Intarsia Designs," in *Interweave Knits*, Fall 2003. Pages 90–93.
—The secret to working intarsia designs in the round.

Høxbro, Vivian. *Domino Knitting.* Loveland, Colorado: Interweave, 2002.
—A basic primer for knitting mitered squares.

Høxbro, Vivian. *Shadow Knitting.* Loveland, Colorado: Interweave, 2004.
—Techniques and designs for working shadow knitting.

Jang, Eunny. "Steeks: Cutting the Edge," in *Interweave Knits*, Winter 2006. Pages 100–104.
—Excellent explanation of the hows and whys of steeks.

Kandis, Mags. *Folk Style: Innovative Designs to knit including Sweaters, Hats, Scarves, Gloves, and More.* Loveland, Colorado: Interweave, 2007.
—A nice overview and tips for working different types of color patterns.

Keele, Wendy. *Poems of Color.* Loveland, Colorado: Interweave, 1995.
—Historical and practical summary of knitting in the Bohus tradition.

Melville, Sally. *The Knitting Experience: Color.* Sioux Falls, South Dakota: XRX Books, 2005.
—A reference for all types of color knitting.

Radford, Leigh. "Knitting in Color: Intarsia Basics," in *Interweave Knits*, Spring 2006. Pages 80–82.
—A basic how-to for knitting intarsia motifs.